LEFTOVER LEFSE
Sagas and Stories

by
Art Lee

Illustrations by
Dee Anne Najjar

published by

Adventure Publications
P.O. Box 269
Cambridge Minnesota 55008

ISBN 0-934860-48-3

To My Publisher

David Nordell

Who was willing to take
the financial risk that
readers would buy books
about Scandinavians.

Leftover Lefse: *Sagas and Stories*

From the Publisher:

This book fulfills with grace, poignancy and humor the goal of the author, Art Lee, to relate in three successive books the tales of what happened to some of the Scandinavian immigrants — and their children and grandchildren — who came to the great Midwest.

First came **The Lutefisk Ghetto** (now in its 9th printing), second was **Leftover Lutefisk** (now in its 4th printing), and now **Leftover Lefse,** which likely shall be as popular as the other two. Interest in ethnicity is very much alive at this time period.

Altogether there were 106 different ethnic groups who came to this country and helped make and make up the United States of America. Some forty-four million newcomers arrived both in waves and in dribbles over a century and a half in what was not only the greatest demographic movement the world has ever experienced but also the world's greatest anti-poverty program.

Of those 106 different people coming to our shores, it is highly significant that Scandinavians made up three of the top four nations in numbers **proportionately** to send their sons and daughters to the new land, Amerika (see **Harvard Guide of American Ethnic Groups**). After the Irish in first place came Norwegians in second; next the Icelanders, and then the Swedes. In total numbers, the Swedes would be the largest of the Scandinavian emigrants with some 1.3 million. There were about 850,000 Norwegians and perhaps 25,000 Icelanders. For each nation mentioned, however, the figure listed represented almost a quarter of that country's population at the time of the mass migration! That's a lot of Scandinavians.

Leftover Lefse presents the sagas and stories of primarily the descendants of these immigrants in this land, this Nation of Immigrants, as President John F. Kennedy labeled it. The tales in this book are sometimes funny, sometimes sad, and sometimes a combination of both, but most certainly they are never dull. Fellow Scandinavian-Americans today will easily be able to identify with the events and characters portrayed, especially if they grew up in a small town or had rural connections. For urban non-Scandinavians? Well, they'll learn about a part of Americana that they never knew existed — and be amazed and amused by the process.

Contents

The illustrator, Dee Anne Najjar . . .
as seen by . . . Dee Anne Najjar.

You Know You're
In A Small Town When . . .

. . . you dial the wrong number and still talk for fifteen minutes

. . . you write a check on the wrong bank and they cover for you

. . . you don't use your turn signal because everyone knows where you're going anyway

. . . the day of your grandfather's funeral the neighbors bring in enough food to feed an army

. . . you get married and the local newspaper devotes half a page to the story

. . . people don't drive to another town to visit, they "motor" their way there

. . . you call every dog on the street by name and he wags his tail at you

. . . some people believe the name of the town comes from the name on the water tower

. . . you miss a Sunday at church and the next day receive six get-well cards

. . . you learn of your daughter-in-law's pregnancy before she does. (The gal who did the lab-work is your next-door neighbor.)

. . . you're not supposed to eat noon lunch until after the fire-siren rings exactly at high noon

. . . the day your kitchen caught on fire you received ten invitations to supper

. . . you drive into a ditch five miles out of town and word gets back to your family before you do

I

Leftover . . .
Late Forties

The Concert That Never Was

It was not an organized quartet, let alone a Barbershop Quartet, the latter category of singers at least knowing what they are supposed to do — even if they can't always do it.

Yet this unorganized quartet, this curious foursome, did indeed sing together, sort of, for about two weeks before a quick collapse. Their moment before their public was blessedly brief.

The men began singing, perhaps understandably, in the local tavern, singing their best, or so they believed, when their larynxes were well lubricated with contents coming from large brown bottles. After sufficient liquid fortification, they sang very loudly, with gusto, accepting the dictum that when in doubt, beller.

Their rehearsal room was the men's lavatory, a safe haven to experiment with their new-found choral structures. Although the group did not last long enough to acquire a name, they spent so much time practicing in the can that they were quickly dubbed "The Latrine Four."

The Four were a strange assemblage, each member a character in his own right. Singing the high tenor was Maurice Manor, and because of his literal manner, he was called Mousie — and his last name usually was pronounced Manure. "Mousie Manure" was a true neck-tie tenor in that when he strained mightily to hit those high notes, it appeared that he was being strangled by his neck-tie.

On the low bass was Wilhelm Sverre Johnson, sometimes called Bill Johnson, but regularly known as B.S. Johnson, whose early fame came from his connections with an area radio station which found him giving the stockyard market reports in an innocent, inadvertent word-styling that gave guffaws to his limited audience. Seldom have the animal sales reports ever been so filled with double-entendres as when B.S. stated his analyses. Sample, and the favorite quote repeated often by the Hardware Store hangerouters: "In today's market, bulls were up while cows held steady."

The melody-line of the quartet was attempted if not sung by Odd Peterson who, despite his already appropriate title, still had his small-town nickname like almost everyone else, to wit, Banjo-Eyes, this because he was somewhat cross-eyed. Years before he was a fairly good basketball player in that he faked so well, the opponents never knowing which way he was looking.

The remaining singing part in a normal barbershop quartet would be the baritone, but that is a tricky part requiring the most skilled musicianship, so pseudo-baritone Hervey Gjertson simply wandered around vocally during each song, joining in with whomever he felt like at the moment, as his muse called him. Hervey, because of his gaunt appearance, had his required appellation too, Scurvey-Hervey, as his mournful, hang-dog look made it appear that the skinny Hervey would pass away from this cruel world before the next sundown.

For two weeks The Latrine Four alternately entertained and/or terrorized the crowd in the barroom on weekends with their caterwauling. The later the hour, the louder they sang, harmonizing on old war-horse gut-busters like Old Mill Stream, Sweet Adeline, and their version of Now Is The Hour — "When We Must Take a Shower."

Their pattern of performance didn't vary. First they'd disappear into the lavatory, then practice, then charge out and bust into songs that fell into the general category of Music for the Vocally Retarded.

Their rendering of some songs was more like pig-rendering, but nevertheless at the end of each rendition, a raucous voice in the crowd would holler at the bartender: "Hey, dere, set up a round for da boyss! Dey're purdy durn good, yew betcha!"

By midnight, with the judgment of both the singers and

the audience considerably impaired, they were wailing at full throttle and ready to make their appearance on Major Bowes Amateur Hour.

And that sudden willingness to leave their confines of comfort for new pastures was where they made their mistake. In a moment of foolish rashness for both the inquirer and inquirees, it was agreed to their singing the following morning in church, filling in at the last minute as a replacement for an ill vocalist.

"Ya durn tootin' we'll sing! We're gona bust chords for those Lutherans like they've never heard before!" yelled B.S. Johnson, confident of the group's new-found abilities.

"Yah-da, den, yew gice'll make dose stain-glass vindows rattle vit yur power," agreed their solicitor and agent. But just to make it seem more churchy, The Latrine Four agreed to have Mrs. Karsten Voie accompany them on the piano while they would belt out "The Old Rugged Cross." Yes-sir-ree, sir, it was all arranged; they'd made their general public debut in front of the whole congregation.

The next morning at 11 a.m., the holiest hour of the week, there sat Mousie Manure, Scurvey-Hervey, Banjo Eyes, and B.S. Johnson in the front pew, each with a clean white shirt on. But already it was apparent that something was wrong. They sat there like zombies, no one moving. 'Spirits' were not moving them in the morning compared to the night before.

Unfortunately the moment came quickly in the service when the pastor announced Special Music "that we don't normally hear in church." It would be abnormal, all right. Slowly, but slowly, with eyes averted, The Dejected Four shuffled up to the front of the altar and reluctantly turned around to face the music, as it were. It was impossible to tell at the moment which one up there was more scared than the others. There they stood, The Frozen Four.

The kindly Mrs. Voie waited and waited for the pre-arranged nod, the signal for her to go ahead and begin the piano introduction. No nod came, each man appeared catatonic. Finally Mrs. Voie felt that something had to happen so she began playing the opening line of the hymn, which was to serve as the intro, after which she pressed the soft-pedal to quiet down as the men were to begin singing.

Mousie looked at the ceiling, B.S. Johnson looked at the floor, Scurvey-Hervey looked out the window; Banjo-Eyes looked somewhere but no one could tell where for sure.

Once again Mrs. Voie played the introduction, this time very loudly and emphasizing the melody line by pounding out the part for The Vocally Impaired Four. Mousie's lips moved to open, then closed quickly to cut off his drooling; B.S. Johnson tried to swallow but his mouth was too dry to swallow anything; Scurvey-Hervey looked wild-eyed at the others and shook his head at their disaster; Banjo-Eyes dug his hands into his pockets and made swerving body motions which said clearly: let's get outahere!

But yet again Mrs. Voie played the opening line, this time very slowly as so to try to coax The Fainting Four into the song that each one knew backwards and for-wards when they were in a more comfortable location — and still no vocal response unless B.S. Johnson's hyperventilated breathing could be counted as sound.

Mrs. Voie then closed her hymnbook. That signal was clear and the men didn't miss the cue. They bolted quickly from the altar but did not go back to their pew. It was out the side-door without hesitation and to the graveled park-ing lot out behind the church. Without stopping, without a word, without even a single good-bye, each got into his vehicle and pulled away in a rush. They also pulled away from any more quarteting.

Perhaps church president Emil Skurvik summed up the general critical analysis of their singing abilities when he informed the men in front of the Hardware store the next morning concerning that aborted rendition of The Old Rugged Cross: "Y' know, dat's da best dey effer sounded."

The Trauma of 'Tag' at the Pickle Station

It was simply called the "The Pickle Station." It was a cucumber-receiving agency, one of dozens throughout the state owned by the firm of Jewett & Sherman, but pronounced locally, in view of their economic practices, as 'Jewm -&- Screwm'.

The pickle station sat on the other side of the millpond but it was only a short distance from main street, and to the station in the late summer came the streams of drooping cars and trucks with their heavy loads of cukes,, all handled by the agency manager who was appropriately named Pickle-Jake both summer and winter.

The major customers of Pickle-Jake were the area farmers, most of whom kept a pickle-patch of small dimension as a chance to pick up a little extra cash for themselves, but often these patches meant a year's bank-account for their kids.

There were a few farmers, however, who devoted large portions of their land to raising cucumbers and those patches required the need of outside help, namely migrant laborers.

Each summer the migrants came into the district and lived in their shantytowns of makeshift housing on the farm where they worked, these housing units invariably referred to as 'Mexico City'. Although the workers were actually Americans — with the license plate of TEXAS on each and every vehicle they drove — they nevertheless were perceived as "foreigners" by the locals.

On the biggest farms the Mexicans came early in the season, first to hoe the cucumber hills, and then later to pick off of the smelly, prickly vines the millions of cucumbers, preferably the little ones — the Numbers One or Two — as Pickle-Jake paid much better for the tiny ones. Large cucumbers, the kind that cost so much in the winter, were simply thrown to the side of the patch in the summer.

In this land of tow-headed and blue-eyed Norskies, the few migrants among them stood out markedly. They were obviously physically different but the incessant wild rumors about them made them seem really different. Despite all the stories, however, the Mexicans lived peaceably and presented almost no significant social problem to either the local community or to themselves.

And yet the rumors persisted and got added to and magnified multifold about how these lean, brown-skinned men with their black hair and big black moustaches all had fiery hot tempers, and short fuses — and long knives! And wide-eyed listeners heard hairy tales of drunken brawls and then knife fights and then stabbings and even murders.

The frightening stories were all very exciting to the children in town — even when they only half believed them — who spent portions of the year playing around the pickle station because it was such a good place to play hide and seek.

In the summer and fall, Pickle-Jake chased them away, but in the early spring the station was deserted and thus open territory for fun and excitement. Especially exciting for kids was to crawl up the tall wooden ladders leading to the tops of the fat wooden vats, those huge holding-tanks that resembled the big wooden-water-tower down by the depot, except that the pickle station vats were usually filled with a thick brine, a stinky substance that reminded everybody of the station's location when the wind blew in a certain direction.

Into the brine-filled vats went most of the fresh cucumbers, there to age, there to literally get pickled, there to stay well preserved for months on end until someone came to remove the converted cucumbers on to the final process, canning.

The early spring was the best time to play around the vats as most of them were empty by then, and kids would crawl up the ladders, peek over the sides and see if they were empty, and if they were, the kids would jump down inside and hide.

Naturally the children had been warned time and time again by their mothers to stay off those high ladders and warnings like that made them naturally gravitate to the vats. Anything that offered an element of excitement was appreciated by the children who figured out very early in life the nothing but nothing of interest ever happened in their poopy home town.

Such was the scene and situation on this warm March Saturday when a group of youngsters swarmed around the empty pickle station ready to start the new season and the first of many games of hide and seek. But they only played one game and never finished that one.

Because Bendic Brekke was the last of the kids to arrive, he was declared by the others as the first one to be "it," and his little pal Shorty Olson knew exactly what he'd do the moment Bendic turned his head to the wall, covered his eyes, and began counting to 100.

Shorty Olson high-tailed it as fast as he could to the closest vat and began shinnying up the half-broken wooden ladder going straight up along the side. As Shorty neared the top, he could hear Bendic's voice reaching number 75, but he figured he had plenty of time to make it. Still huffing and puffing, Shorty got to the last rung and swung one leg over the top of the tank before turning to look inside. He looked, and then he froze.

"Ninety-seven, ninety-eight, ninety-nine, one-hundred!" hollered Bendic; "here I come, ready or not!" and he turned around to search for his hidden comrades and was startled to see Shorty Olson just sitting there on top of the vat, one leg in and one leg out.

Bendic turned back quickly, touched goal, and shouted the proper words: "One - two - three - I - see - Shorty." He added "Jeepers, Shorty, you're sure slow hidin'."

Shorty managed only to get out a faint "C'mere; c'mere!

C'mon up here and see what I see. It's just layin' there."

It was the tone of the voice more than the words that made Bendic realize that something was very wrong. He ran to the ladder, pulled himself up beside Shorty as quickly as he could, then got out a "What is it?"

"There, in there! Just look for yourself!"

And there it was, a body floating face down in the pickle brine, arms outstretched, just bobbing there like a cork in thick water, the black handle of the knife sticking out between the dead man's shoulder blades.

The sheriff and some deputies came within the hour and removed the well-preserved remains of the Mexican. Nothing more was every heard about the case.

Sam's eating habits were bizarre . . . yup, yup, yup . . . .

When Eccentrics Were Simply 'Town Characters'

We have lost our appreciation for poor and even middle class eccentrics. In other words, if you're not too well off today and act "different," you're quickly labeled as crazy. Only the rich nowadays can aspire to eccentricity and get away with it.

It wasn't always that way, thank goodness. The town characters in our lutefisk ghetto just following World War II were not thought of as psychotic; they were, well, just sporty individuals acting . . . ah, naturally.

We had the most marvelous eccentric, a harmless screwball named Sam Hellum. Today his antics and general life style would bring in the county welfare worker and three psychiatrists, but in the time of Sam's heyday he was just a wonderful character.

Tall, lean, toothless, ageless — fiftyish — with a sunken face and brown eyes that made him look like a mournful hound-dog, Sam lived all alone in a twelve by eight foot shack out in the woods south of town. It was at home that his "differences" could clearly be noted. He slept on oak planks between two mattresses. The place was heated in winter by four kerosene lamps, one in each corner. He kept a pet snake in the cupboard. The front door opened on the lock-side, the hinges having been removed. Other than the above, the place was semi-normal.

If Sam had a work specialty, it was that of a woodcutter. He especially hated work, however. Work is the curse of the drinking man, and Sam drank a lot. Indeed, he would drink all day and all night if he had the money. When he ran out of bucks, it was back to the woods, double-bitted ax in hand. The ax was his companion, his friend, his collateral.

And yes, Sam regularly got corned or skunky or bombed — and went on toots — but he was the happiest, mellowest, most cordial drunk ever encountered. He never bothered a soul whether drunk or sober or somewhere in between.

Everybody liked Sam Hellum. But he was hard to understand as he spoke a combination of English and Norwegian and sometimes a mumbled dialect so esoteric as to be labeled "Hellumese." A few wags asserted that Sam had the answers to all the world's problems; it was just that the answers couldn't be understood.

And Sam talked a lot. At times he talked steadily — mainly to himself. He held all-night conversations all alone. Almost every evening Sam could be seen lolling on a bar stool, there carrying on a lively discussion with himself that included contorted facial grimaces, head nodding and shaking, and wild gesticulations; and when somewhere in the midst of this one-man dialog, he scored a verbal blow, his hand came down solidly on the bar to make his point more demonstrably, the gesture was followed by his standard admonition of "Yup yup yup."

The biggest mystery surrounding Sam Hellum was how he could stay alive. How that man managed not to freeze to death in the winter-time remains a puzzle and a minor miracle. Night after night after night he would stumble out of the taverns at closing time into a frozen street where it could be twenty-five degrees below zero, and everyone knew that Sam on his rubber legs would not be able to make the five miles to his shack.

Everyone also knew that he slept all over town, whether in abandoned cars, in outhouses, under porches, in granaries, haymows or chicken coops, anywhere he would not freeze to death. (He once offered an opinion on how not to freeze: never lie down in the snow; always stand up.)

Sam's eating habits were as bizarre as his sleeping accommodations. Nutrition was not a part of his vocabulary. (It was primarily a liquid diet that kept him going anyway.) To illustrate, Sam was once given a large fresh blue-gill in the morning and Sam promptly stuck the fish in his top bib-overall pocket, the tail hanging over the side. Sam and the drooping fish, sat all day at the bar until supper time at which point Sam went outside, wrapped the blue-gill in newspapers, lit them on fire and the flames died out, ate the fish and pronounced it to be delicious, albeit a little on the rare side.

To outsiders, of course, Sam was a suspicious specimen of homo sapiens, the stereotypical village idiot to be tolerated but avoided. Not so with the villagers who knew him well, knew he was no dummy, actually liked him, and in some ways respected some of the things he did.

Aside from Sam's joviality, people also liked and admired him for his honesty. He was completely and totally honest. Any money borrowed from anyone, be it five cents or five dollars, would always be repaid at some point, although repayment often took months, and most people who had loaned him money would be surprised at being repaid, having forgotten all about it. "Yup, yup, yup," he'd say and laugh at their forgetfulness.

When Sam had to borrow Big Money, like twenty bucks, he went to the bank and the cashier always gave him the loan even though his only collateral was that double-bitted ax - and his word, which was a bond as good as gold.

When it came to giving money away to kids seeking candy, Sam was the softest touch in town. When it came to coins for little children, Sam practically tithed. It was warmly strange then, and seems even more curious now, that the person in the village who could afford to give away the least ended up giving away the most.

Sam did get his rewards, usually in the form of free beer. He could and would have drinks bought for him all day and all night — and sometimes all morning — by itinerant customers dropping in the tavern for a snort or two. It was an expected ritual of brewery-welfare for the ordering customer to tell the bartender to "set one up for Sam, too."

At times Sam might have a dozen large schooners of Pabst's finest sitting in front of him, an amount that for most people would be impossible to consume, but for Sam quantity was no problem. All he needed was time — and he had lots of that — and Sam would soak up that sauce easier and faster than a toad. "Yup, yup, yup."

No one really knew Sam's background. Recent inquiries today about his origin resulted in the villagers giving only vague information, with the regular response being to the effect that Sam was . . . heck, he always just seemed to be around. Like Topsy he just grew. In interviews most of the locals agreed that Sam had emigrated from Norway sometime, somehow, somewhere; one lady was reasonably sure that Sam had once been in the Norwegian army, which seems suspect, given Sam's disposition and his experience in the American army.

Sam was indeed in the U.S. Army briefly, very briefly, during WWII. In the fury and furor of the wars in Asia and Europe, and the great demand for more American troops, lo and behold and uff da but Sam got drafted and shipped off to Fort Lee, Virginia, where he never made it through basic training because the communication problem between the army and Sam was insurmountable.

Basic training was a disaster because Sam paid no attention to orders. When the battalion was practicing marching and the drill sergeant shouted "Company, HALT!" — Sam kept right on marching. When the Sarge yelled "ABOUT FACE!" Sam kept right on marching. When the three-striper shouted "COMPANY LEFT!" Sam kept right on marching straight ahead. Even worse, he was always out of step.

It wasn't that Sam was uncooperative, let alone incorrigible, but he just wouldn't/couldn't/didn't follow orders. The greatest danger to his fellow G.I.'s in Fort Lee was not the Nazis who might be shooting at them some day, it was Sam shooting at them at the moment.

Sam Hellum was issued an M-1 rifle — an aberration

quickly regretted and immediately rescinded — but not rescinded before Sam had banged away indiscriminately in every direction except that general region where the targets were located.

A fellow townsmen who coincidentally happened to be in basic training along with Sam was asked in an interview about that debacle. The man shook his head in wonderment as he recalled Sam's misbehavior, declaring that Sam in the U.S. Army was a scene right out of Sad Sack combined with Abbot and Costello and the Three Stooges thrown in, with Sam playing every character. Trouble was, Sam wasn't acting, he was for real and that reality spelled chaotic disaster. "Yup, yup, yup."

So the Army let Sam go home, mercifully for everyone. The Army even gave him a set of false teeth before sending him on his way, but the teeth he lost when he got off the train at Baltimore and went on a toot.

Yet it turned out that that brief moment of madness in the military literally would save Sam's life. By the 1960's Sam's misused body, heretofore immune from cold to colds to cholera, could no longer snap back after a week's debauchery; the old joints didn't come around after sacking out in the rumble seat of an abandoned Model-A behind the Welding Shop.

Compassionately, both of the town's tavern operators — both men who shared a mutual affection for Sam — ran the errands, made the phone calls and readied all the legal arrangements for Sam to be admitted to the national Veteran's Home in King, Wisconsin. After all, Sam was a veteran of sorts, even if the men in front of the hardware store had proclaimed that Sam wouldn't be called into military service until Minneapolis was invaded.

So Sam lived out his remaining years at King, there sleeping between clean sheets and getting three square meals a day for the first time in his life that anyone could remember. There was some doubt at first whether his body could adjust to the dramatic changes. Soon a marvelous rumor spread that after Sam had been there for about a month, he began complaining about the cold drafts coming under the door of his bedroom. That rumor sent the locals into paroxyms of laughter.

Sam is gone now, but the stories about him still go on and folks still do imitations of his mannerisms, ending with "Yup, yup, yup," and then lighting the wrong end of a filtered cigarette in his honor.

Today the Sams of the world would be called crazy; back then he was just thought of as a wonderful character. Most certainly he was truly a free person who lived each day the exact way he wanted to. Just maybe he did have the answers to the problems of the world. Are only goofy people honest? Yup, yup, yup.

(For Photographs of Sam, see p. 197)

Hymn to Lutefisk
(Tune: "O Tannenbaum")

A Song for the Musically Retarded, The Vocally Impaired

1. O Lutefisk, we bow to thee,
   The king of all the fishes!
   Thy flaky flesh soaked soft in lye,
   How fragrant and delicious!
   We wait each year for thy return,
   With wat'ring mouths and hearts that burn—
   O Lutefisk, thou hast us hooked;
   We cannot live without thee!

2. O Lutefisk, thy subtle taste
   Beats any Deutsche flavor -
   No wienerschnitzel, sauerbrat
   Can ever win our favor!
   Who'd every touch mere kraut or wurst
   If "Norway's pride" were tasted first?
   O Lutefisk, no German food
   Can take thy place among us!

3. O Lutefisk, it must be said,
   No dish is more celestial!
   When heaven catches wind of thee
   It envies things terrestrial
   All bathed in butter, or in cream,
   With hearts a-flutter, eyes that gleam,
   We do adore our Lutefisk,
   It's more divine than mortal!

Written by a German convert to the
"Loyal Order of Lutefisk Lovers"

The Revenge of the Chicken Pluckers

Every town has its strange characters, of course, but it's still wondered why our Lutefisk Ghetto was blessed with such an inordinate number of them.

To illustrate, we had an assorted pair of misfits, a father-son team of chicken-raisers, and those two guys could have made anyone's list of all-time-characters.

The father was Hans senior and the son was Hans junior, but in view of both their ages and sizes, the elder was always referred to as **Stor** (Big) Hans and the grown son as **Smaa** (Small) Hans.

Although Hans & Son lived on a farm, of sorts, they owned no farm vehicles. All they had for transportation was a '47 Ford and this vehicle served for all purposes. For example,when the men came to the co-op with a load of grain, the grain was all piled high to the ceiling, the back seat having been removed. It certainly was different indeed to watch Stor and Smaa Hans shoveling ground oats through the smashed-out back window of a four-door Ford.

They also hauled Holstein calves in the back seat, but what the poor car mainly served as was their chicken-truck. When the men rode off to town to trade — literally trading chickens, live or dead ones and some half-way in between — the '47 Ford looked like a chicken coop on wheels. It was a sight to behold.

Squished into wire-mesh crates were live chickens and the crates were placed on any surface of the car that would hold a cage or two of the squawking, squalling, feather-flying white leghorns. Thus there were chickens covering the entire roof of the car, chickens on the fenders, chickens on the hood, chickens on the front and back bumpers, and chickens tied to the door handles on both sides.

(This moving chicken-coop led to many curious stares, and it was always confusing trying to tell who was driving, what with all the chickens. One day when the chicken-car came squawking by a neighbor's farm, the neighbor called out to his hired man who was standing near the road: "Who was at the wheel? Stor Hans or Smaa Hans?" And the reply came back: "I don't know, all I could see were chickens.")

The chicken-men were harmless enough and didn't disturb many people, nor were they bothered in turn by others — except for this one time when they got mad at the local depot agent who ticked them off.

The agent — a crusty, surly sort of guy — had offended the chicken team by not having the train stopped at a certain place where it would have been more convenient for them to unload some produce — and reload some chickens. The depot agent was an ornery, independent cuss — and he wasn't even a Norwegian which automatically made him a suspicious outsider — who didn't give a hoot in a rain barrel how he treated his customers, let alone those two ding-bats Stor and Smaa Hans.

But this time the agent went too far in his cavalier behavior. Said the father to the son, or so it was reported: "Vell, den, ve'll show dat bird hver da bear vent in da buckwheat," or words close to that.

Revenge was promised, revenge was planned, revenge was carried out, and their plan went perfectly. The smell lingered for weeks.

There was to be this special day when the train was to stop with some extra cars to pick up a huge mound of potatoes owned by a big-nosed, big-shot dealer who was liked about as much as the depot agent. The event was important enough for the railroad regional boss to be there to make sure that everything went smoothly because there was a time-factor involved in that there was a limited amount of time in which to get all the potatoes loaded and the train off on a side-track before another train was due to arrive from the other way. Timing was crucial.

Stor Hans and Smaa Hans took care of the timing. The train was to arrive just at dawn, but the night before the chicken tycoons had worked for hours and placed on the rails all and every form of chicken parts available, especially chicken fat. Just around a sharp curve, and out of sight, for 500 yards down the track all the steel rails were covered completely with gizzards and guts, feathers and fat, bones and beaks, chicken-heads and chicken-rumps.

Anyway, all the big shots were there when the train puffed towards town to pick up the precious potato cargo in the allotted precious time. The train engineer slammed on the brakes early, but the train did not stop where it was supposed to; in fact it didn't stop at all. The entire train literally slipped and slid through town, past the depot and on down the tracks for a good half mile before finally coming to a halt. Then trying to back up the cars with all that chicken crud on the wheels caused for more delay so that the whole pick-up-plan was ruined for that day and delayed for a week.

The depot agent was mad, the regional boss was mad at the depot agent, the big-nosed potato dealer was mad at both of them. Had all these angry people not been so busy standing there shouting and trying to finger the blame on each other, they could have looked up to see an old white '47 Ford gliding slowly away from the scene of the crime. It wasn't really white; it was just that all the chickens on top made it look that way.

The moral of the story: treat chicken pluckers with more respect.

Applied Christianity Acts in Curious Ways

"Show me the manner in which a nation cares for its dead, and I will measure with mathematical exactness the tender mercies of its people, their respect for the laws of the land, and their loyalty to high ideals."

Wm. Gladstone

* * * * * * * * *

On a ridge overlooking the wide valley stood the Updahl Lutheran Church. Standing in a straight line across the lush farm valley on the other side of another ridge stood the Rochdahl Lutheran Church, a white-frame building almost identical to its counterpart on the far horizon.

Between the two institutional landmarks lay the patch-work quilt of farms of the solid citizens who were almost all first and second-generation Norwegian-Americans. They were so very Lutheran, went the common saying, that in their valley it was a common belief that there were only two kinds of people: either Lutherans or heathens. And among the latter category, of course, lay Roman Catholics, that was for blame sure. In the nearby community just over the ridges the religious views were fully as extreme. On Sunday mornings the Lutherans walked down main street eight-abreast on their way to 11 o'clock service while the scarce town Catholics in their lowliness slunk down the back alley to 6 a.m. Mass. Ecumenicism was a fancy word that didn't exist in this farm region.

* * * * * * * * *

Ole Toftum drove his matched pair of Belgians down the edge of the field. It was a familiar chore, one that had to be done every fall, but Ole Toftum loved fall plowing. Even after many years he still thrilled at the sight of the shiny black dirt rolling magically forward like some long-stringed earth-snake coming forth from the earth's depths.

This day Ole Toftum planned to guide the horses and gang-plow and stop them somewhat short of the fence line in order to leave more habitat for the pheasants. That's what he planned, but to his puzzlement and embarrassment he drove the critters right against the fence and the surprised horses stopped immediately. What had happened, he wondered, to make him react so slowly? He had seen the fence coming up in plenty of time; he just didn't respond quick enough. Somehow his hands didn't act right.

After supper that night Ole Toftum stood at the dry sink getting ready to shave, all in preparation for him and the missus to go to town for trading, and also to take in some doings that his kids were in at the local high school.

He pumped the hand-pump just fine and got water into the gray dish-pan, but when he picked up the straight-edge razor to scrape off the day's stubble of whiskers, his arm wouldn't raise right. It was like the whole arm had gone dead on him. He also started to feel a bit faint and sick to his stomach, so he decided to lie down on the couch.

When Ole Toftum woke up from a nap, he couldn't move off the sofa. The numbness that was in his arm had moved to both legs. Then, and only then, did he call his wife and tell her what was happening.

A hurried call to the doctor, another call to the ambulance, yet another quick call from the doctor to the Mayo Clinic led to Ole Toftum being rushed to Rochester.

It was too late. Ole Toftum, age 50, died the next morning from a large tumor on the brain. He left behind him grieving wife and six young children, the oldest a boy of sixteen.

He also left behind him a heavily mortgaged farm, a herd of Holstein cows to be milked by hand, thirty acres of corn yet to be husked and brought into the corn crib, and a winter poised to descend in a fury upon the valley.

The widow was distraught, depressed, confused, disoriented, unsure; she did not know what to do or where to turn. But her neighbors knew what had to be done — and they did it with no hesitation. Before the cruel winter descended on the Toftum place the neighbors descended there ahead of it.

The neighbors took care of everything - from the funeral to the corn to the Holsteins; from the fall-plowing to the winter-wood supply to the storm-windows; from the initial funeral hot-dishes to a year's meat-supply, to the weekly visiting and whist-games.

And the help and concern never stopped; both the aid and the months stretched out. Ongoing help literally kept coming to the Toftum family for years afterwards. The neighbors saw to it that the kids learned how to run the farm — profitably — and yet not miss one day of public school. And three years later when the oldest boy ended up getting drafted into the Korean War, well then the next boy got his special training from the neighborhood.

So the mother kept her farm, stayed there in the valley, raised her children, and eventually, years later, when all the children were grown and had gone — and had made their choices not to farm - she rented the land and moved to town to a retirement home.

This story could end here, but there is one significant point that needs to be added: Mrs. Toftum and her children were all Catholics. Amid that sea of Lutherans lay this one island of Catholics, the only 'heathens' in the valley. Yet in that ocean of prejudice moved even stronger currents of human decency and kindness.

Today the Updahl and Rochdahl Lutheran Churches still stand there, still loom high ever the rich farm valley lying between them. Today it is both dumb and also a bad joke to suggest that there are only Lutherans or heathens. But then the Toftum family found that out forty years ago. Sometimes applied Christianity acts in curious and marvelous ways.

Mons would go down in the verbal runestones
as being the winner . . .

Mons Monson
vs.
The County Judge

Modernization came dramatically to Hitterdahl township. Well, it seemed not only dramatic but also both emotional and very modern then — County Trunk Q got tarred.

County Trunk Q had begun as a pioneer corduroy road, then slowly evolved from mud and wood to mud and gravel, then to limestone-gravel, then pea-gravel, but even with the combined ingredients, the road remained a quagmire in the spring, a dustbowl in the summer, and a combination of ruts and ice in the winter.

The decision of the township board members to black-top Q was a major undertaking, each member regarding himself as a tighter Norwegian than the other guy. The competition in that category was fierce.

But they voted to tar despite the pain in the pocketbook, despite the vocal opposition. And there was opposition! Local orneriness concerning the new road came out in several forms but none was a more deliberate rebellion than that of Mons Monson who thought the whole idea of black-topped roads to be not only expensive but downright dumb, a disgrace, a blot on the land, and an invitation to mobile madness.

"Hitterdahl's Route-66," Mons named it. "Effrey hot-blooded speeder in da county vill take it fer da Indin-aplis speedvay, den," Mons declared and added the obvious: "An' a perfect vast uff money."

Not that Mons could not afford to have his taxes inched upward as Mons was perceived as one of the richer — as well as peculiar — farmers in Hitterdahl valley. As the men in front of the Hardware Store observed, "Dat Mons Monson; hees rich, but got a sca-rew loose in hiss head, den."

Mons was not one just to sit and whine about what he didn't like, the way most of the Hitterdahl folk did. He took action! — and some action it was indeed. Mons showed his disdain for the board, his contempt for the road, and his willingness to face any legal consequences by deliberately driving his huge iron-tired Fordson tractor — a monstrous, belching machine with six-inch steel lugs — across the newly tarred road to get to a forty on the other side.

To add insult to injury — and turn a narrow strip of the new road back into gravel again — his Fordson pulled as big disk-harrow behind, the disk weighted down with anvils and ten-gallon milk pails filled with cement. (When Mons wanted to make a point, he was not one to go about things halfway.)

Such open defiance, such obvious destruction, indeed mutilation, of County Trunk Q brought down the wrath of the town board who promptly arranged for the contemptuous Mons to be hauled into court.

It was a memorable trial, albeit brief and to the point. When the county judge asked Mons if he did what they said he did, Mons answered firmly: "Yew bet!" which response the judge ascertained as meaning in the affirmative, and he promptly fined Mons one hundred dollars.

This pronouncement of the judge then led to a curious exchange between the court and the defendant, an exchange which will be remembered in the community for several generations hence.

As soon as the judge rapped his gavel and thundered, "One hundred dollars!" Mons immediately replied: "Yew better made dat tew-hunert, Mr. Yudge."

"Huh?" grunted the judge, taken back. "Why two hundred?"

" 'Causs Aye gotta git dat damn stuff back 'cross da road agin."

The judge began to sputter and look for a way out. "Well . . . er, can't you arrange to have your tractor and disk returned to your farmyard on a truck and trailer?"

"Ya-shewer, Aye could do dat. But Aye don't vant to. So dere, poot dat in yur pipe and smoke it."

"Mr. Monson, your recalcitrance and general attitude make me want to fine you double that first amount."

"Go, 'head, den. Yust remember dat Aye got a lot more money dan yew do."

The latter premise was not to be determined; neither the judge nor Mons were ready to haul out their checkbooks and compare balances. For that brief moment in history, of course, Mons had probably lost, but in the annals of Hitterdahl folklore, Mons Monson's contribution to the ongoing saga of stubborn Norwegians would go down in the verbal runestones as being a real winner.

How Marriages Become Unhitched

Theirs was not a marriage made in heaven. It might have been made in. . . that other place. What held Bertel and Gladyce Johnson together was the slender thread of guilt caused by some solemn vows made at their wedding. It was an agreement made in haste, said Bertel later, but he agreed grudgingly that he had indeed made a promise, of sorts. Contracts can be very binding, including marriage contracts.

Then, too, what also held them together were the prevailing community mores, an added Commandment, the local pressures which said loudly and clearly: "Thou shall not get divorced! Thou shalt live with that monster to the end!"

"Til death do us part," they had mumbled twenty years ago. Their marriage had died the following year. After one year of connubial bliss, they barely tolerated each other, except when out in public, at which times they put on a show worthy of an Academy Award.

Privately Gladyce regarded Bertel — "Lout," as she was wont to call him — as the laziest man "in da 'hole vide vorld," and for good reason as Bertel had never lifted a finger in twenty years to do a single thing around the house. "Ladies work." he sniffed; "men do real vork."

Bertel would not so much as cooperate even when Gladyce was in the middle of her housework. For example, when it came time to vacuum the living room rug, Bertel would not even lift his big flat feet when the noisy Hoover approached the big lunk sitting sullenly in his easy chair. So she had to go around the chair, around The

Great Stone Face studying the **Look** magazine.

That chair by itself was symbolic of Bertel's disgust for his spouse, too. Thanks to "Ol' Horse Face" — as he thought to call her but never did dare say it out loud — his beloved easy chair had been totally covered with fancy crocheted doilies and knitted covers and towels to the point where the original chair could not be seen. All those confounded doo-dads made Bertel's stomach retch. Then too there was their ornate parlor organ in the corner which Gladyce wouldn't even let Bertel sit at, let alone play. No doubt the marriage was coming to an end. They knew it — and so did the whole town. They weren't fooling anybody with all their public play-acting, but it did make for great theater.

"Ay vant to be fair 'bout dis, Bertel," said Gladyce, still imbued with her second-generation accent. "Ay hope da Lord comesss an takes vun of usss. Den Ay kin go an' liff wit' my sister."

That moment almost came. It was an incident that maybe didn't break the camel's back but it ended forthwith their marriage. It happened on a Saturday morning as Bertel was preparing to haul a trailer-load of garbage and junk to the village dump. He didn't quite make it. After this occasion, he would locally be forever known (behind his back) as "Trailer-hitch Johnson."

That fateful morning Bertel had his small two-wheel trailer loaded and was about to wheel it up to the back of his Chevy when he saw that the hitch was broken. The ball-joint had snapped off and needed to be welded. Yet with everything loaded and ready to go, he hated to delay the trip, and besides, the dump on a Saturday morning was a great place to visit with people. He could see folks at the dump that he hadn't seen in ages, or at least a couple of weeks.

Bertel decided he had to go and he devised a make-shift plan which he carefully explained to a bored Gladyce: "I'll open the trunk and sit inside and hold the trailer-bar while you drive." This scheme seemed safe and reasonable, he believed, especially after he warned her to drive slowly and carefully — and be very easy on the foot-feed when accelerating.

So off they went, very carefully, very slowly easing out of their driveway, Bertel crouched in the open trunk hanging on tight to the trailer bar and Gladyce behind the steering wheel. Momentarily it seemed as though the plan might work after all.

It was after car and trailer came to a halt at the stop sign off the main highway that both the plan and their marriage literally came apart. For reasons known to Gladyce — but with the whole town speculating on it afterwards — she suddenly pressed the accelerator to the floorboard! The car shot forward and Bertel shot backward! Out tumbled the surprised, jolted body of Bertel into a rolling, falling heap on the highway. Insult to injury was added as the trailer ran over him before veering off into the ditch where it overturned, spilling garbage everywhere.

When the half-stunned Bertel lay in the middle of the road groaning and cursing and shouting lines of non-endearment at his evil wife's sadistic behavior — "GLADYCE! YOU'RE LOWER THAN A SNAKE'S TAIL IN A WAGON RUT!" — the wife drove blithely down the highway, totally oblivious and presumably unaware of the miserable mess behind her. But there was a smile on her face.

"Trailer hitch Johnson" filed for divorce on Monday morning.

Little Chivalry
at a Shivaree
(but lots of fun)

Among the more curious rites once connected with Scandinavian-American weddings was a post-nuptial event called a Shivaree.

A generation ago shivareeing was a common custom; at this writing it is less so, and perhaps it's just as well. Present day brides and grooms may be better off with one less party foisted on them so suddenly at the start of their house in the middle of the night.

And yet shivareeing was great fun for everyone! Well, maybe not quite all; it was less fun for the ones being shivareed, namely the new wedding couple.

For the reader who is uninitiated, a shivaree was, by loose definition,a kind of impromptu party for newlyweds, a surprise party (at least it was supposed to be a big surprise), an occasion marked by semi-planning as suggested by many phone calls made around the countryside a few days before the bash with words to the effect: "Hey, then, we're gonna shivaree Nels and Annie tomorrow night. Wanna come along? Should be a dandy!"

The crowd of well-wishers would assemble at a pre-arranged place and time, all the participants armed with raucous noise makers, usually homemade. The group would then sneak up to the newlyweds' home in the dark of night, completely surround the house, and then at exactly the same moment, they'd all make the loudest noise possible!

The initial shock waves inside would usually scare the poor wedding couple half out of their wits, and only after several seconds of wondering if the end of the world was near — (and the surprise assault was often marred by loud giggles and guffaws of some merry-makers) — would the couple realize what that infernal racket was all about and relax enough to follow the next expected rule of shivaree-ing, that is going outside to welcome their noisy, uninvited guests into their honeymoon home.

The rules didn't stop there. The poor groom is next sup-posed to furnish sufficient quantities of drinks for the thirsty dishpan-pounders, wash-tub-thumpers, bucket-bangers, siren-ringers, horn-tooters, and whistle-blowers. So the requirement for the spanking-new husband is to hustle off to town and return quickly with plenty of sauce, namely a case or two or three of beer if there are only a dozen revelers, and if there are more in the mob, then it's to be a couple of ponies and/or a sixteen gallon keg. Whatever, the rules require that one does not run out of beverages!

Meanwhile the new bride in turn is to search the cup-board shelves and breadbox for vittles enough to feed this ravenous crew once they have consumed the suds and are actually considering the possibility of leaving the house and returning to their own homes.

Shivarees could last into the wee hours of the morning, regardless if the groom had to be at work the next day at 7 a.m. Any hint to that effect would be answered the same way: "Ah, then, whadaheck, your're young! You can take it! An' you can sleep next winter. 'No rest for the wicked.' 'Sides you ain't sleeping much these nights anyhow. Ha ha ha!"

For a few of the locals in our Lutefisk Ghetto, shivarees were highly prized and anxiously awaited events, pri-marily loved by those impecunious souls who saw shivarees as a grand opportunity for a Big Night Out — for free! These financial conservatives could hardly wait for a happy couple to get back from their honeymoon before nailing them with a bar bill. (These less than great spenders [read Tightwads] were said to have their wallets and purses inhabited by moths, the latter species in reference to how often their money-bags got opened.)

Some citizens simply gloried at the opportunity of a bachanalian festival funded by a new husband who could ill afford any extra spending, let alone sums for frivolities for the stomachs of thirsty friends, neighbors and acquaintances. Coming to mind is a remembered line of one such cheapskate bibbler: "Happiness is still feeling thirsty after drinking six bottles of beer."

Another remembered line — even shuddered at in those days — involved the constant desire of at least one shivareer to make the married couple's life memorable by placing a pound of Limburger cheese on the manifold of their car's engine, the eventual smell of which would be enough to drive a skunk out of its den! This was going a bit too far for most of the party-goers and almost always the perpetrators would get talked out of such a rotten, literally, scheme. After all, fun is fun, but hot engines and stinky cheese go beyond fun; that's awful! That's downright cruel!

Of course shivarees were a great occasion to exchange local news and gossip, often phrased in the local slang. Example: "Hey, den, did yew hear dat Kjitel Kjendalen iss sittin' tight in da Court House? 'Course den hiss ol' man sat fast dere hisself long before dat nincompoop kid did." Translation: both father and son spent time in the county jail.

Naturally the newest stories would be told with great glee, especially those about Swedes, the latter being the butt of most jokes: "Hey, then, did you hear this one? The Easter Bunny, Santa Claus, a smart Swede and a dumb Swede were all equal distances from the chimney. In a race to get there first, who won? (Pause) Give up? The dumb Swede will arrive first because there's no Easter Bunny, no Santa Claus, and no smart Swede. Har har."

What would start as a friendly, desegregated, intermingling affair between men and women would invariably end up with all the men in one part of the house and all the ladies in another, the latter usually in the living and dining room and the former in the kitchen — all the reason to be closer to the ice box. And woe be to that bold creature who dared to "integrate" either grouping. There may have been no written rules but there were sure plenty of unwritten ones, so that any man who dared to join his wife in the living room for over sixty seconds was deemed a wimp or worse. Not even the poor groom would be tolerated to be with his bride. There's "man-talk" and then there's that other silly stuff that only women of both sexes talk about, and certainly He-men will have none of that!

Eventually the party would wind down; eventually the yawns would start along with frequent glances at a fat silver pocket watch coming out of bibbed overalls; eventually the talk would turn to the cows waiting to be milked in the morning for some, and that Long Drive into town for others; eventually everyone would go home, almost all leaving within five minutes of each other. When one couple started it, the rest picked it up in a hurry and pulled out too. Come together, leave together, fast.

And eventually during the leave-taking — among the "god nats" and "takk for matens" and "tusen takk for oel" (good night, thanks for the food, many thanks for the beer) — participants could expect the wise Hjalmar Pederson to lay on a bit of his folk wisdom to the bridal couple, whether they wanted to hear it or not. Hjalmar, almost illiterate, was wise and clever in many years of observing the human condition. He didn't talk much, but when he said something, it was worth listening to. Hence his parting remarks to Nels and Annie:

"Vell, den, yew vill know ven yew iss gittin' old hven da kinda pressents yew got fer yur vedding iss being sold in antique storess."

Peasant knowledge, stories, fun, food, booze, good neighbors, good people; they all came together at a Shivaree.

Kids Never Stop Doing the Darndest Things

Ten-year old Edvard Nissen was a special child. Full of life, full of spunk, full of snoose — and certainly full of the devil. And yet he wasn't really a bad kid, it was just that he liked to play tricks on someone, and that someone was his poor mother, a grass-widow, Agnes Skrutholdt Nissen.

Poor Mrs. Nissen. Thanks to son Edvard, she was one big bundle of nerves, a walking psychiatric case, a nervous-Nellie whose entire skinny body seemed wound as tightly as the rubber-bank Edvard's Spitfire balsa-wood airplane, the one he flew from the rooftops downtown to buzz and attack his unsuspecting mother walking on the sidewalks down below.

Because of Edvard's energies and antics, Agnes Nissen seemed just one step from entering the funny-farm. "That kid'll be the death of me," was a more than routine cliche uttered by a million other parents; in Agnes' case, the wal-ed remark was an absolute truism. Certainly Edvard seemed to work constantly at her mental demise.

Everybody knew about the jittery Agnes. The old men hanging around the hardware store corner had their own perverted mischief in mind whenever they saw the distraught woman hurtling by them. Each man would then dare the other to give her an early Christmas goose — just to watch her being the first lady to fly over the treetops on her way to the moon.

Anyway, there as this one hot dog-day in August — a stultifying hot day when all the kids were solemnly warned by parents never to go swimming or they'd get polio for sure and likely to die. Edvard and Gang were playing and were poking around in the back alley behind the combined Furniture-Funeral Parlor store when what to their mischievous eyes did appear but an old abandoned coffin lying there by the garbage can waiting to be tossed into the village dump.

With the sighting of the coffin came the clear message to Edvard and Gang: it was time to have a funeral! With black crepe paper for arm bands, with the coffin mounted and somewhat balanced on a child's wagon, with a proper corpse planted inside the coffin (his face was floured for effect), the young mourners set off down the street to conduct services in the village square for their fallen comrade, just the way the big folks did it.

The children played their roles to the hilt. One boy even turned his shirt around backwards to obtain a clerical-collar effect, all the better to preach a sermon. And so the tender-aged congregation was all assembled on main street to conduct a children's ersatz Norwegian Lutheran Requiem Mass of sorts for a dear friend who at the moment was finding it awfully hot and difficult to breath with the coffin lid closed.

A choir of three was singing "Holy Holy Holy" when shopper Agnes Nissen emerged from the store carrying two large grocery bags under each arm, and she spied the gathering of kids and of course the funeral bier around which they were gathered.

"What's going on, children?" said Mrs. Nissen, a bit warily.

"We regret to inform you that . . . well, we really hate to have to break the news to you this way, Mrs. Nissen, but . . . well, our dear brother disobeyed orders and he went swimmin' in the mill-pond and sure 'nuff he caught polio and . . . and, yup, he did, he croaked right there on the spot. And we know now he should have listened to you, but —."

"LISTENED TO ME? WHAT DO YOU MEAN? WHO'S IN THERE? I DEMAND THAT YOU OPEN THAT UP RIGHT NOW YOU LITTLE BRATS."

"O.K., Mrs. Nissen, but I don't think you're quite ready for the shock. But there he is," and the cover flipped back revealing a very dead-looking young lad lying serenely inside.

"EDVARD!?" was the only audible word she could say as both grocery bag contents flew in all directions.

"Hi Mom!" piped Edvard, sitting up straight, but Mom never heard the cheerful remark. She had fainted dead away.

Poor Agnes Nissen, the men with the white shoes kept coming closer to her every day of Edvard's young life.

Rural Phone Operators Knew All

Time was not that long ago when a person planning to make a phone call first began by giving the crank sticking out the side of the phone box on the wall one sharp turn of the handle. That crank-maneuver was to get one in contact with the operator so that within seconds the caller could expect the telephone operator to respond in her practiced flat-voice with her patented word, "Yallo."

The lady did not say "Hello," or even "Operator." The non-word "Yallo" combined in two short syllables all the lines necessary for her to indicate "Good day. This is your operator. I am here to help you. Who do you want to talk to?"

After that first "Yallo" came the caller's directions to the operator which never followed those of the phone-book. The person was supposed to give the proper phone-book number of the party to be called, something like "Please ring for me 78 R-2-2-1," so the operator could immediately plug in the proper line before she gave a small handle on her switchboard some pushes resulting in household number 78 hearing two short rings followed by one long ring on the multi-party phone line. That was the proper procedure, phone company rules.

Nobody followed the rules. Instead after the opening "Yallo," it went "Hi there, Daisy, gimme Teman Peterson," and the operator, Daisy Dybdahl, was supposed to come up with Teman's number from the top of her head and ring the house forthwith and no hesitation. And she could and she did.

Any phone operator worth her salt on the rural lines

knew everybody's phone number. It was expected, part of her job; it went with the territory. Only a novice substitute tossed in briefly would not know the numbers by heart and in one hour's time the unknowing sub could manage to upset most Scandinavian callers when she'd ask the crank-ringer, "What is the exact number you're calling?" Such an impertinent question would lead to: "Jeez, I dunno. Couldja look it up for me?" And she could and she would. (If she wouldn't, she wouldn't have her sub job very long.)

Rural phone operators performed extra duties far beyond connecting two talking parties. They provided the weather reports, knew the starting times of all local social functions and where they'd take place; they knew who was at home and who was away — and for how long; they knew not only who was in town shopping but also which stores they were in; they also knew who was in the taverns and were expected to call the taverns for the wives who refused to call the taverns themselves.

In effect, they knew all the news — and then some. The nature of their job allowed them to know what was going on and where, if not, why. They simply knew more because they were in a position to hear information. Sometimes they heard more than they should ever have known! In these cases they were expected to be priest-like in not divulging confidential information — but sometimes the news was so hot and so good that it slipped out anyway. (Being a close personal friend of an operator let one in on the world of choice, juicy gossip. No wonder they had lots of friends.)

The interaction between rural operators and callers was extraordinary, and yet this intermediary role was expected. For example, when two talkers got to jabbering too long on a party line, the operator was expected to step in and cut them off, but to do so in a manner so diplomatic as to win her a Nobel Peace Prize.

Operators, when not busy, were also expected to spend time visiting with lonely people who just needed somebody to talk to: "Daisy, I just had to hear a human voice. Lemme tell you what went wrong today . . ." And Daisy was a good listener.

Operators were even expected to "cut-in" on conversations when their special expertise would be beneficial, but in this otherwise "nosiness" operators had to intervene in a manner that made them appear devoid of any personal interest in the conversations. Sample: "Yallo, just heard that the Ladies-Aid meeting at Selma Vik's house has been changed to Tekla Bekadahl's place, and it's Thursday, not Friday. Just thought you'd want to know." And the ladies did want to know and appreciated the information.

On occasion operators had to make judgements that might have seemed impertinent if not dangerous, for example calling the sheriff's department for immediate action after an inquiry came via a phone call from a tiny child wondering where his daddy and mommy were as they didn't come home during the night. Or a quick call to the one and only cop in town after hearing raucous voices outside on the street and looking out the office window to observe an unruly crowd gathering outside the tavern at 1 a.m. with two major antagonists in the middle waving fingers at each other.

Much indeed was expected from operators, including patience. Year after year they had to grit their teeth and put up with the same prankish kids' phone calls to the local grocery stores, each generation of children hearing for the first time the stale joke that the operators had heard when they were eight years old, too. "Hello? Storekeeper? Do you have Prince Albert in the can? Y'do? Then for heaven's sake let him out! Hahahahahahahaaaaaaaa." More patience was yet required from would-be Scandinavian comics trying out their latest story from the telephone operator: "An' den, Daisssey, ven dose Vikings inwaded Scotland, den, dey knocked da pants off dose guys! Hoo hoo hoo."

Yet proper courtesies were expected of callers to their operators, too. For example, when the fire siren rang its howling, mysterious wail, everyone knew that the operator at that moment was notifying all of the firemen in a "conference call." This took two minutes. Only after that elapsed time was it then acceptable to ring the phone crank and ask breathlessly, "DAISY, WHERE'S THE FIRE?"

Callers were also expected to make no phone calls after 10:30 p.m. unless it was an absolute emergency. In another sense, anyone who received a phone call after the bewitching hour of 10:30 just knew that it had to be something BIG! (They also knew that they had gotten the operator out of the bed/cot beside the phone-exchange panel board.)

As to making long distance calls late at night, well, this required the messages to be on the verge of calamitous! Either getting or giving a long distance phone call after midnight just screamed the word EMERGENCY! (Any operator who didn't listen in on these calls was really shirking her duties; her friends would never forgive her.)

Not everyone could be a telephone operator. There were requirements that were written, but more important were the unwritten laws. For example, one had to be female, forty-ish, preferably unmarried — and given to wearing one's hair in a pug.

None of those "rules" were written down, of course. Some gals didn't want to become operators because of the unwritten "rules." To illustrate, alas, those ladies who accepted a full-time position as a telephone operator at the same time made a semi-public statement to the effect that they'd be spinsters for life. The two jobs seemed to go together: alone in the office, alone at home. Such was the high price to be paid for the honor of saying "Yallo."

Rural phone switchboard operators have today gone the way of the bustle, the Ford V-8, and Swing-and-Sway-With-Sammy Kaye. Like the latter three items, operators were once an important part of America, and more so. After all, they knew all the local dirt! Today people have to resort to rag-sheets like the **National Enquirer** to get the dirt on national figures, but who cares about far-away figures like Rock Hudson when you could find out via the phone lines that Palmer Moe's hired man was doctoring two towns over for some strange social disease? Now that's news!

"Yallo." A word to be heard no more from an American institution, the rural telephone operator.

Norwegians Do Not Know How to Drink

Every community regardless of its size has its share of town characters. Little seems to change along that line. Village officials today still shake their heads in wonderment and disgust, believing that their particular community has been unblessed with a disproportionate number of citizens who too often behave so strangely.

Fitting into this general category of characters would be the town drunks. Our Norwegian-American community had them in the 1940s; they're still around in the 1980s, and the term "characters" seems appropriate for those thirsty souls who call public attention to themselves.

We had some lulus! And we laughed long and hard at them at the time because we were school-age kids who thought drunks were funny. Our parents knew better, of course, and they perceived those same persons in their drunken condition as pathetic, disgusting, and a disgrace to themselves, their families and the community.

To illustrate, we kids perceived Torben Jacobsen's week-long toots as highly entertaining. Torb would regularly act like a dog and crawl around the downtown streets on all fours while mournfully howling at the sky. Most adults would click their tongues at this same scene and deliberately walk across the street to avoid the baying Torben in the sauce.

We students knew even then, however, that Torben fit into that special class — and there were others like him, too many it seemed — who could not take just one drink and stop. If a whiskey bottle was opened, it had to be finished; the drinking didn't end until the bottle was drained.

That kind of drinking pattern led naturally to the point of extreme intoxication resulting in victims' actions and behavior that even we smart-alecky high school kids would wince at. For example, Hans Hokesvik once got so drunk that when he went out to the pig-pen, he fell in among the pigs and lay there in a numb stupor while the pigs ate portions of his body. Thank goodness the hired man found him in time and actually saved Hans' life.

There were enough men like Torben and Hans who simply could not drink in a civilized manner, as the phrasing went at that time, so even then people asked the big WHY. **Why** can't these Norwegian-Americans stop after one or two drinks? And from this question came the obvious query: Is it mainly Norwegians who suffer from this malady?

That last question used to interest me when I was a young man in our Lutefisk Ghetto; in later years the question intrigued me, and now it bothers me because the issue is still very relevant both in America and Norway.

It is no kept secret that Norway has had in its past and still has today an extraordinary problem with alcohol. One need only to be in the public parks of Oslo about sundown when almost a magical wave of the wand finds stumbling drunks emerging from the shadows of the trees to stagger forward and fall down on the grass.

A couple of years ago when I attended some classes on Norwegian culture at the University of Oslo, the question of Norwegian drinking habits was put to the lecturer, a Doctor Welumson who was a top director in the National Health Service. Upon hearing the question, Dr. Welumson first put his head down on the desk in front of him, then he raised up and answered simply: "Norwegians do not know how to drink."

In the next half hour, Dr. Welumson discussed the alcohol mess in Norway and made a number or observations: "Ordinary Americans drink more than Norwegians, but Norwegians get more drunk."

He explained: "Norwegians normally do not have a daily drink before meals; instead they drink heavily on weekends and on holidays. But once they get started, they don't know when to quit." (Again I thought of the Torben Jacobsons, Norwegian-Americans who fit the doctor's description perfectly.)

Dr. Welumson said that there is not proportionately a higher number of alcoholics in Norway than America or western Europe. He believed there were more alcoholics in France, for example, where, he said, people commonly die of liver problems caused by too much drinking. But that is not the situation in Norway where people instead will sometimes die from brain damage caused by an excessive amount of alcohol consumed at one time. He then shook his head in perplexity and disgust, then said: "I cannot explain WHY Norwegians drink the way they do. It may be some cultural flaw, but it is not genetic. The problem seems to have no answers."

In his concluding remarks, Dr. Welumson stated that one way the government had hoped to reduced heavy drinking was to charge exorbitant amounts for all liquor (a bottle of whiskey, for example, costs about twenty-five dollars), but he admitted that even the high prices did not improve the situation. He then mentioned that along with the willingness to pay high costs of booze from the state-run liquor stores, most Norwegians can and do buy a common, cheap moonshine liquor called **hjembrennet** (literally Home-Burned), which is mixed with coffee or anything else, and it's 195 proof!

At the very end of his comments to his classroom filled with Americans, Dr. Welumson apologized for all the drunks we should expect to be seeing in downtown Oslo and in the city parks during our stay.

His prediction was accurate; his apology was unnecessary; his information was interesting, fascinating, even if the answers were not there. The question remains, Why?

Baseball, Bravado, Buffoonery and Bravoes

There are basic do's and don't for baseball player behavior during games. A certain ritual is expected and accepted by fans and players alike, and woe be to the malefactor. These unwritten rules apply to participants whether it be in the big leagues or the bush conferences, whether the game is played in the Minneapolis Metrodome or a cow pasture ball field at some four corners.

Player violations of these semi-sacred rituals do happen, of course, and such non-conformity itself becomes newsworthy. An occasional player does upset the apple-cart, producing results that usually bring embarrassment and disgrace to the player, his team, his family, his whole community. For example, from the 1985 World Series, about all that's remembered is the boorish behavior of a few St. Louis Cardinals.

And yet a rare few players can get away with what would normally be labeled as outrageous behavior. Not only can these special iconoclasts pull off their stunts, they can walk away heroes! To win this latter designation requires the player to have the right stuff and the timing must be right.

Both the times and the personality were right in an extraordinary game played on a Labor Day weekend following the end of World War II. "The times" then meant a national period of joy and celebration that followed the ending of the world's worst war. Finally, but finally, the killing had stopped; the war was over, and the boys in military service were returning home almost daily, and

By George, Ma, this is the funnest game I've ever seen . . .

they were happy beyond description to be back safely.

Such was the wonderful moment for this young, handsome ex-G.I. just out of the Army, and so delighted was he to be home and free and ALIVE that the combination made him just exude happiness. This energetic, bright and gifted youth also happened to be a superb baseball player. Indeed, a few old-timers who had watched a couple of generations of players regarded the young man as the best natural athlete ever to attend the local high school.

His skills were welcomed. The local town-team had been invited to play the featured game at the County Fair, the sponsoring Fair Board attempting to pit the two top regional teams for the benefit of the Fair's biggest crowd which always showed up on Sunday afternoon, a crowd that both understood and loved good baseball — and loved to witness a good grudge-match too.

This forthcoming Labor Day weekend game was more than a showdown between two hated rivals, it was a longstanding rivalry that was in no small way an ethnic fight; in effect it was The Norwegians versus The Polish.

However, the two teams were not evenly paired and the Norwegian team manager despaired at the expected drubbing his charges were to receive unless, of course, some minor miracle occurred. The miracle did occur, in the form of this kid just out of the Army, his fresh discharge papers in his back pocket and that ruptured-duck pin on his jacket collar telling the world he was a civilian again.

And Lars — which was his nickname — was glad to be asked to play for the locals at the Fair. But are you in shape? wondered the manager. "You bet. The Army made sure of that," he answered. How's your baseball skills? "Well, maybe a little rusty, but a couple swings and a practice ground-ball or two, and the eye, the arm and the swing'll be there."

Lars then added something the manager couldn't quite understand: "We'll likely win the game, but either way we're gonna have fun. At least I aim to have a good time. You may not get this, but I'm a free man! and well! and

ALIVE. You gotta understand how great it is to be home! I tell you we're gonna have a ball at that ballgame!" In response to all of the above the manager was perplexed and suspicious. Turned out he had good reasons for his suspicions; turned out that he'd be so embarrassed that he'd be looking for a hole to hide in.

It was time for the game to begin, but then there was a delay grudgingly tolerated. It was a brief flag-raising ceremony in center field, the local high school band tootling out the Star Spangled Banner, and the p.a. announcer asked everyone to sing along. Nobody sang. Like mutes, the grumbling crowd stood there impatiently shuffling from one foot to another, no hats removed, no hands over the heart. There was no hint of glory for Old Glory.

At last the ballgame was underway when the snarling umpire yelled "Play Ball!" His manner denoted there would be no toleration of any shenanigans; the first guy that lipped off at him would be shouted back in his place; the first guy that deliberately bumped into another player would have his rear-end tossed out of the game. It appeared to be that kind of a mean contest.

Lars, however, led off and came up to the plate grinning; it was the only smile in the whole ballpark. He had said he'd have fun and he meant it. Meanwhile the manager found out to his chagrin about his suspicions. The first pitch to Lars came in wide of the plate, and he responded vocally and loudly with mock seriousness:

"Now, Pitcher, I want a ball I can hit, not one way outside. Get it over! O.K.?"

"BOOOOO!" began the crowd, heretofore sitting quiet and bored. "Get that bum outathere!" hollered one fan. "Deck that show-off!" yelled another.

Another pitch, another ball over the plate, but low. "C'mon, Pitch," said Lars loudly, pretending to be disgusted. "I want a pitch not too low, not too wide, but right down the middle of the plate. All right?" And Lars smiled widely enough for the whole park to see.

"BOOOOOOOOOOOOOOOO!" roared the crowd, suddenly stirring to life and finding their darker nature at the same time. In front of them was this smart-aleck defiling all the proper rules of baseball decorum. And worse, he was obviously enjoying himself doing it! "DUST 'EM OFF! GIT THAT SHOWBOAT!" screamed a red-faced spectator, appearing near apoplectic with rage. "Obliterate that dumb Norskie!"

Lars' teammates were looking sheepish and the poor manager was mortified. Two teammates in the dugout began looking for something under the bench. In the bleachers Lars' father suddenly found it necessary to get up and go check on something in the car while Lars' kid brother pulled up his coat collar on this warm day and pulled his head and neck down like some retreating turtle.

Another pitch, this one in the strike-zone, and WHACK! Out screamed a clothes-liner that should have gone for at least a triple, but running halfway to second Lars stopped completely, turned to the mound and announced: "Now that's just where I wanted it, pitcher. And I thank you. But now I must go," and he just walked slowly to second base and stood there grinning like the proverbial Chesire cat. Then he shook the second-baseman's hand — and did a little dance.

Some fans laughed, and a few hollered approval, but the great majority just booed raucously and roared their disapproval at this shameful behavior. What's this all about, anyway? A joke, or somethin'? This is serious business! It's supposed to be a grudge-match; the players are supposed to sneer silently and hate each other like good ballplaying Americans should.

The crowd was working itself into an ugly mood over this . . . this traitor! They could hardly wait for the guy to get into his shortstop position where they could verbally ride him unmercifully and most assuredly cause him to bobble every other groundball. They were increasingly on his back with ferocity and meanness. They'd show that smart-ass Norwegian kid a thing or two and shape 'im up. Damn Scandinavians!

Yet at shortstop Lars fielded brilliantly. His was an extraordinary fielding performance. Absolutely flawless.

Because of his strong throwing arm he could play deep-deep at short and he made plays from behind second base, saved grounders that the third baseman had missed, and still throw out the runners. Moreover, he ran like a deer to catch would-be Texas-leaguers as well as sprinting way past the foul line to catch balls no one dreamed could be catchable. His playing couldn't be faulted - and he was having such fun doing it all!

Back at homeplate it was the same vocal patter: "C'mon, Pitcher, gimme a pitch I can reach. Now is that asking too much?" Then followed the Boo-birds yowling amid vulgar epithets normally not heard in public places. But then he'd nail another pitch, blast yet another linedrive, then stop along the way to thank the pitcher and stroll along and stop at second or third where he'd wave at the pretty girls in the stands in a section where he suddenly acquired an immediate fan-club. And always he smiled and laughed, and it was obvious to all that Lars was having just one whee of a good time. It was becoming impossible not to admire him if not like him.

Gradually the crowd began to get caught up little by little to what was going on. They could sense the situation, see the pleasure; could realize that it was a rare kind of ballgame, that it was indeed just a game, a game to be enjoyed. It wasn't really a grudge-match after all, just a ballgame between a couple of local towns on a pleasant Labor Day weekend, a weekend to get out and meet friends and have a couple of beers while enjoying the great American sport of baseball. The Great War was indeed over and our America had indeed won it, and wasn't this a great country after all? And now our lads were coming home from this awful war and they were so happy to be home and physically well and so darn happy to be back — like that goofy kid playing shortstop who's reminding everybody what life is all about and how short life really is and what pleasures should be taken from living each day.

What began to happen next was beyond belief. Soon the crowd, both teams, and even the umpire got caught up in the spirit of fun. The man-behind-the plate began to change his brusque style; his prior formal, clipped pronunciation of "strike" turned into a mock-theatrical "streeeee-aaa-rrrr-i-keh-keh-keh," to which sounds the crowd responded with guffaws of laughter and howled their approval of this once-mean-man-in-blue.

By the last innings everybody was having such a good time that it didn't seem important who would win. The mood became festive. The early adversarial-relationship between the two teams had broken down to the point where the players were spending equal time in each other's dugout. In the bleachers everybody began visiting with everybody.

The early angry, yea verily near-psychotic, screams of invectives hurled at Lars at bat and the no-fooling cries of "STICK IT IN HIS EAR!" had led to the crowd — the WHOLE CROWD — chanting in unison: "We Wanna Homer!" We Wanna Homer!" and they got one. In his last time at bat, Lars belted a waist-high fastball over the center field wall. Then he stopped between second and third to doff his cap and laugh and throw kisses and laugh some more and soon the whole crowd was laughing and cheering him on to even more highjinks!

It wasn't a game anymore, it was a party, a serendipity party that all there were sorry to see end. By then Lars' father had come back to receive strangers' handshakes and hear remarks to the effect that "Yes sir, that is quite some young man you got there, Yes-Siree-Sir," and people were telling each other that "By George, Ma this is the funnest baseball game I've ever been to in my whole life!"

By then Lars' kid brother had long ago emerged from his coat collar to yell to the whole world: "That's my brother! Ain't he great! He just got home and out of the Army Air Force, and he was a top turret gunner in a B-24 and he was in Germany . . ." and the kid didn't need to say the obvious: he's my hero! And the little kid was so happy and so proud of his big brother that he could almost bust.

The game did end, darn it. The once mean-spirited grudge-match between the Norwegians and the Poles had turned into a love-fest. Afterwards the players, the fans, families, the crowd — heretofore perfect strangers — all mixed together in a happy social spree amid handshakes and hugs and huzzahs all around and good-natured kidding — and the quaffing of large quantities of what the Polish called "peva" and the Norskies called "oel." It was beer all around.

It was a wonderful crowd scene. For this brief, poignant period of history in this faraway town at this faraway time, a warm, wonderful moment-in-time showed its head briefly and everyone there sensed it. The people continued to mill around the park until nearly dark, and as the last of the sun's rays struck the American flag high on the pole in center field, a quiet hush fell over the crowd but no one needed to say a word about the message; yet the feeling was there and the message was clear.

For a brief instant we were struck with a palpable surge of patriotism. We knew clearly that we were all Americans, not Poles or Norwegians or even angry players and cursing fans. That simple sermon was felt deeply. All were again reminded that it is the little things in life that count the most after all, and it is little things like a minor ballgame at a County Fair that will be remembered firmly, fondly forever by those people who were there.

And all because of a friendly, exuberant and talented ex-G.I. called Lars who was simply happy to be home and free and alive. His feelings were infectious.

Addendum: Lars, of course, was my big brother Loren, and I was the little kid alternately ashamed and then elated. The game described remains one of the most memorable of all athletic contests ever witnessed. Loren would continue after college to play summer baseball and was several times chosen "Player of the Week" by the Minneapolis **Tribune** in the 1950's, a decade when Sunday town team competition was still the biggest event of the week. At this writing Loren lives in Northfield, Minnesota, where he manages an employment agency.

When he returns to his boyhood home to visit the Lutefisk Ghetto, he is invariably reminded by somebody of that particular game. To one hometown fan, retired for several years now, who has been literally to a thousand games played by everyone from big league pros to little league tikes, that County Fair game remains the sporting-experience of his lifetime. It was quite an event.

For photographs of Loren/Lars Lee, see page 196

Ahhhh! Mmmmm! Chicken Every Sunday

Rural traditions develop for many reasons, some of them prompted by the technical progress of the times, or the lack thereof. Among these country folkways was the eating of fresh baked chicken in the hot summer months for every Sunday dinner. It was both a practical thing to do and sort of the proper thing to do. Indeed, it was perceived by many persons that farm wives who did not serve chicken during the Sunday noon hour were neglecting their expected duties. Sunday and church and chicken somehow all went together then.

Time was not that long ago when American farm homes were devoid of artificial refrigeration, a time when preserving foods in the summertime meant either canning, drying or salting the products, when butter remained temporarily non-rancid by sealing it inside Kerr jars which then floated in water in some large ironstone crock down in the cool cellar below the house, that gloomy, dirt-floored dungeon reached by carefully winding one's way down some steep wooden steps below the trapdoor in the corner of the kitchen.

Without proper refrigeration, of course, getting fresh meat to eat in those hot summer months meant that the choices were limited to small critters like ducks or lambs or fish — but there was always chicken. Ahhhhh, chicken! It graced thousands of farm-home platters following the 11 o'clock service at the local parish church.

There were rituals in the church services. Preceding holy rites there were other rituals at the farm homes followed just as carefully, patterns to follow leading to those marvelous moments tasting succulent drumsticks, breasts, and wings — and what can be better than chicken gravy?

The Sunday ritual began with Grandpa Lars — an emigrant from Laerdal, Norway — arising before dawn and going immediately to the chicken coop to gather the eggs, and at the same time determining which of the lovely leghorns babbling quietly in their nests would be the chosen ones that morning to grace the round-oak dining room table that noon.

The martyrs once selected, Lars then headed for the pumphouse where he kept the double-bitted ax, his hand-wielded guillotine with which to administer the coup de grace. As the sun chinned itself on the horizon, Lars, with ax in one hand, would dip a tin can full of water out of the cattle tank and then make straight for the big round grindstone sitting next to the machine shed. With the dripping water-can hanging on a wire above the grindstone, he'd sit in the rusty seat and begin peddling the simple machinery which would get the heavy stone turning in a smooth and steady motion. The ax blades would then go gently down on the revolving wet wheel making a hissing sound as edges on the blades were hones so sharp that he could shave with them.

When satisfied with the sharpness, Lars would lumber back towards the chicken coop — an old log building that had once served as his first farm home following his move to the once empty land — and then came the stalking of his quarry, eyeing each wary bird as one by one they edged forward through a tiny opening in the hen-house wall leading outside into the new daylight.

Lars may have been in his 70's and long past his mobile days, but when it came to grabbing chickens, he was quick! With one swoop downward of his still-strong arms he'd scoop up one squawker by the legs and with another dip and swoop he'd come up with his second made-for-dinner leghorn.

The neat nabbing of two chickens inside ten seconds was done with grace and artistry, but watching him shuffle off with two frantically wing-pounding, leg-jerking victims which seemed hysterically aware of their fate was not a scene of beauty, especially knowing that they were heading immediately for the chopping block, a three-foot tree stump just off the outside cellar door of the square, white, wood-framed farm house.

The executions came immediately. Down came the ax once and up flew a headless chicken; down came the ax again and off to the side rolled and jerked yet a second headless wonder.

And that ended Grandpa Lars' portion of the ritual. Now Grandma Julia took over. She was already there beside the chopping block, ready and waiting with scalding-hot pails of water beside her. The birds had scarcely stopped twitching before each was immersed into the steaming buckets, and then the feathers flew with strong bony hands and fingers plucking and pulling at the carcasses. Back into the buckets and back out for more denuding until with five minutes both birds were as shiny and smooth and hairless as a baby's bottom.

With the outside slick and clean — which included a singeing with a rolled up **Decorah Posten** set on fire — came the part of the program for internal surgery. A couple of deft cuts with a paring knife were followed by no-nonsense hands disappearing into the cavity and reappearing with entrails dripping, items quickly dropped into the slop-pail nearby. The only inside parts saved were the gizzard, liver and the heart, items regarded as delicacies and both the regular causes of fights at the dinner table by the grandsons when it came time to divide the birds fairly and squarely on each one's hot plate.

With the inside pocket cleaned out, the pungent-smelling stuffing went into the empty cavities. The cloves,, the breads, the chopped-up onions and liver added a spicy aroma that would be enhanced even more when the prepared birds hit the hot oven of the Monarch kerosene stove sitting ready and waiting in the summer kitchen.

The creaking oven door would be quickly opened and inside was gently placed this heavy, black cast-iron pot, the snugly fitting lid hiding the two plump birds which would emerge later browned and cooked and so edible when the family got back from church at noon. Just the thought of what's-for-dinner made the church services go that much more quickly. And of course there'd be mashed potatoes and sweet potatoes and jellies and beet-pickles and home-made hot rolls and after all that stuffing of the stomach would come the urgent but difficult decision of whether to have apple or lemon pie for dessert. Somehow gorging at Sunday chicken dinners seemed the proper thing to do.

Today there is scarcely a housewife who comes close to ever removing a single chicken feather, let alone going through the whole ritual from chicken coop through super-market packaging. And even easier — no touching required — there's immediately available Colonel Sander's Chicken, or Broasted Chicken or Southern-fried Chicken, but there is still nothing to match the taste of the truly fresh chicken, that was once served in thousands of farm homes in the days prior to refrigeration. With that point in mind, in some ways, those were 'The good old days.' And today?

Well . . .

> Mary had a little lamb
> The lamb began to sicken
> She shipped it off to Packingtown
> And now it's labeled 'Chicken'.

Dropped Drawers,
Drooped Jaws

— and pure guts

The men who sat in front of the hardware store were a motley outfit. They looked harmless. There were harmless. Yet many ladies in town found them intimidating.

Each day in good weather the dozen men gathered outside the hardware store on main street just to visit, some sitting on the short cement ledge sticking out from the store, some perched on the fenders of cars and trucks parked in front, others sitting on the cracked cement curb with one leg up on the sidewalk and one in the gutter, the latter an area where many of the ladies thought the men's minds were.

Just the presence of these men bothered many women, including Clara Vesle who proclaimed to her nodding neighbor that all the men liked to look at her legs. This premise would be debatable as Clara was 75 years old and had skinny legs as roundly bowed as some cowboy who lived on a fat horse. In a greased-pig catching-contest, Clara Vesle wouldn't have a prayer.

Because the hardware store was next to Karl Jorgen's grocery store, it was difficult for women shoppers not to have to walk by — and usually through — the small congregation-in-overalls gathered together for daily pro-gnostication.

Some women deliberately avoided the men by taking the long route around them, crossing to the other side of the street a block away and then making a long loop and coming to the store from the other way.

The men never once openly intimidated a single female

passing by. In a strict sense they did not vocally bother anybody, unless stopping conversation altogether while a lady strode by could be interpreted as "bothering the women." There were no snide comments, never any whistling, and very few smirks. Yet just the silence of the group was unnerving. Simply walking past the hardware store was viewed by some women as running-the-gauntlet.

What if something awful happened just then? What if the worse thing that could happen would happen right there in front of all these . . . these naughty men? And what was the worst thing? To have your panties fall down, that was the worst of the worst.

Would or could this tragedy ever happen? It did happen. It happened to Alvina Fuglestad. Alvina was a middle-age farm lady of considerable girth, what in more delicate phraseology would be called fleshy, but indelicately called just plain fat. Alvina was indeed big and fat - and strong. She had arms like hams and the grip of a vise. Not one man in the tavern wanted to arm-wrestle Alvina. She'd make a wimp out of 'em in two seconds flat.

Alvina was strong of temperament, too. Good thing for her as she had to be strong-minded that day she lost her drawers while walking by the hardware store.

Like many practical women in these Depression Years, Alvina sewed her own clothes, including underclothes, the latter made from flour sacks, the evidence of this made perfectly clear when her huge bloomers lay there on the sidewalk with the stenciled name of Big Jo Flour still clearly visible.

Alvina had come to town in the family pick-up and parked it down in front of the post office, laying out her shopping route carefully, because when she planned her route, there was no change; she blundered forward like a bulldozer even when and if the elastic in her pants snapped. Nothing stopped Alvina.

She lumbered first to the bank, then down to the co-op, then back to the post office and finally the last stop would be Karl's grocery store. The men had seen her coming for a block, saw no hesitation in her step, saw absolutely no change in manner or appearance. And yet all the time her pants had to be sliding down farther and farther.

The timing was such that Alvina had just reached the hardware store door and at that exact moment, down fell the panties, but in this disaster she never missed a step, never looked right or left, never said hell or hello. The pants simply dropped while she kept on marching and whirled into the grocery store. Were it not for the evidence lying there in large quantity, the men would never have known.

What to do? What to say? What would Alvina say? She said nothing. In less than 30 seconds Alvina was out of the grocery store and carrying a 50 pound bag of Big Jo Flour in front of her with one hand, carrying this big sack as though it were a tiny paperbag of children's candy. Looking straight ahead, Alvina again strode through the male assemblage where she deliberately stepped on her lost pants, caught it on the toe of her foot, and flipped it into the air where she grabbed the cloth with her free hand and kept right on walking, never missing a step.

It was a magnificent performance. Such grace and artistry. Such guts! A few men felt like applauding. In a moment Alvina was gone, the pants were gone, the scene was over — but the story would live on forever.

Proper Preachers
Perceived by Postmaster

There are three major topics for discussion in small rural towns: the weather, the school, and the church. Without them, what would there be left to talk about? to complain about, to draw the conclusion that the country was surely going to hell in a hand-basket?

No one person in the community knew more about all three topics or had more depth of feeling towards them than the local postmaster. He knew everything! Everybody! He knew all the dirt! And what he didn't know for sure, he made up. Over 50 years he had developed strong opinions on all these three basics-in-life, and his concluding opinion on each was not particularly positive. He knew where the country was heading — and citizens better bring some ice along.

On the topic of the church, his negative notions could border on the apoplectic, depending on his mood (did he have a good B.M. In the morning?). Given the right listener on the other side of the post office windows to whom to fulminate, the issues in The American Lutheran Church could raise his blood pressure to the popping point as one by one he would tick off those nasty newest changes that so ticked him off in the first place.

Now getting that new red hymnal with its new songs and new liturgy was bad enough, indeed, "a cross to bear," as he phrased it. After all, the old black hymnal had served Sunday folk steady and well since 1917. Why in tarnation should they change things? It's only 1967! For sure the old hymns were better (the good songs had been left out altogether!), the old liturgical church service was better, the old altar gathering dust in the outdoor storage shed was better. Besides, all those items were paid for, and what can be more important than that? Do these new, fresh-faced kid-ministers think that money grows on trees?

The Postmaster thundered on: "The old preachers we had were much better than these recent whippersnappers just of the seminary. What kind of fool notions do they teach 'em in St. Paul, anyway?

"And what had that last young smartass joked were "The Seven Last Words" of every congregation? Oh yeah, these words: "We've Never Done It That Way Before." And then he had the gall to laugh, and preachers ain't s'posed to laugh even if they're not dry behind the ears yet."

When the postmaster got roiled and on a roll, all customers coming in for their mail just had to stand there and listen impatiently to his diatribe. No listen, no mail. Lend an ear — and don't interrupt.

"Yes-indeedy, the old **prests** (pastors) were surely better and that's that. Why? They were dedicated men of God because they were 'called'. And being called meant that . . . well, ah heck, it meant their employment was dirt cheap.

"Ah, the good old days," sighed the postmaster. "Those old salaries were practically nothing. And that was proper. After all, one is supposed to suffer in this world, right? And preachers should set an example on how not to concern oneself with material goods. No money, no temptations of money; so peanuts-for-the-pastor."

On this topic of pastoral pay, the U.S. government representative offered his own brand of theological humor: "The pay ain't much, but the long-range benefits are great. Heh heh heh."

His major rationalization for peanuts-pay concerned housing. "Look, the man gets a free parsonage to live in, don't he? Well, don't he?" The fact that the ancient parsonage was a drafty, old, unheatable barn with 14-foot-ceilings and tilting wooden floors with an attic filled with mice in the winter and bats in the summer could be a positive plus for the preacher, reasoned the P.M. Shucks, all those things can remind The Rev. what the real world is like and take his mind off heaven for a while, which location is probably the coast of southern California, anyway.

Two things about the then current (1967) minister — "this new guy" — really gnawed at the postmaster, the way the man dressed so casually and the way he actively participated in all local social functions. The man unnerved everybody just by his being there. For example, God-by-proxy at the Community Hall whist contest was too much to take. And worse, he knew the card-games well!

The former pastors in years back had been practically recluses, which was just what the townspeople had wanted. "This new guy" showed up everywhere just like, well, like he was a real person or somthin'.

Everyone in town had always admired the local pastors — from a distance, the farther the distance the better. Outside of the church building itself, congregational members felt ill at ease in the presence of a man-of-cloth. In the church and up in the pulpit any preacher was just fine, but the same man coming to visit a home made the homeowners uncomfortable.

Whenever "this new guy" showed up at somebody's doorstep, the greeter would give him a big, hearty - and false - welcome, then open the door widely and say loudly to the malefactors inside: "THE MINISTER IS HERE!" This warning meant there was just a few seconds to hide the beer cans, change the TV channel to the educational station, and slide pornographic magazines like **The Enquirer** under the davenport and replace it with **U. S. News.** Only after this short interval for social disinfectant inside was it safe to invite him in. "Yeah, c'mon in, Pastor, an' have a cup of coffee, then."

Inside the house the strain continued. The same congregational members, who could nod their head in church at some Biblical point made in a Sunday sermon, would practically freeze up solid at the serious mention of

Christ's name in their own homes.

The deity was a term mumbled mechanically before every meal in the most standard, banal table prayer: "Come, Lord Jesus, be our guest . . ." but the mumblers wanted neither the Lord nor his active Lutheran disciple on earth to show up in person at the dinner table. Either one would spoil the meal. Ministers are to be heard in churches and not seen outside them.

It was during the middle of one of the postmaster's standard orations on the decline-and-fall of Western Civilization this one morning when it happened. In the middle of a sentence, "this new guy" came literally running into the post office. The young minister was wearing cut-offs, a dirty sweatshirt with his elbows sticking through the holes, a pair of beat-up tennis shoes, and his big-toe was sticking through. He had about a three-day growth of beard, disheveled long hair, and he was munching on an apple.

He ran to his mail-box, opened it quickly, grabbed the contents, and whisked outside again with a big grin on his face, leaving the shocked onlookers with a full-mouth, one-word semi-sentence: "Hi-ya."

The poor postmaster about died on the spot. Had there not been anyone in there to vent his spleen on, he likely would have died, too. "Wussn't that awful? Wussn't that disgraceful?" was all he could manage to get out. Although the vocal intonation indicated these were questions, there was no doubt about the imperative nature of each outburst.

"See what I mean? I tell you again that our church is going to perdition!" And once more he repeated: "Wussn't that awful? Wussn't that disgraceful?" as though he couldn't believe his first reactions were sufficiently verbalized.

He then caught his breath to add, "I tell you that Reverend Larson would not have been caught dead looking like that," which was true. And Reverend Sovde before him, why that wonderful man wouldn't come to town to get his mail unless he had a white shirt, tie, and suit on," which was also true. With a sigh of remorse, he asked: "Could anything be worse than this?"

It could indeed as the pastor suddenly reappeared in the doorway and announced: "Oh, by the way, Father Mulroney will be helping me perform a wedding next month. It will be the first Lutheran-Catholic ceremony in our church. Isn't that wonderful! Well, gotta go again, but I thought you'd like to know. 'Bye."

No, the postmaster really didn't want to know. He just put his head down on the counter and didn't move, while the rest of the customers tip-toed out the door. Some eruptions are better to avoid.

The Short Lived Career of Sverre Hetadahl in the Building Trades

Sverre Hetadahl had all the makings of a good carpenter. Even more, he literally had all the tools that a carpenter needed, a whole shed full of the newest and finest in carpentry.

Recently out of the U.S. Army and home from World War II, Sverre was ready to launch his new profession in the building trades. It would last one day.

Actually, Sverre was rather skillful with his hands and fairly competent with a hammer and saw. Moreover, the motivation and drive were there, along with good health and the love of working outdoors.

Given all these factors, Sverre Hetadahl should have been a fine carpenter, but he wasn't because of a major problem: he could not read blueprints and, even worse, could not even read a tape-measure correctly. Those little markings on a ruler threw him for a loop.

When it came to seat-of-the-pants measuring, where the lovely words, "about" and "approximately" could be the determining factors on where to saw a plank or where to cut out for a window-frame, then Sverre's work was adequate, even if the results were a bit skewed.

However, when people actually got fussy enough to want a window panel exactly at right angles and in the right spot, too, according to the architect's drawings, Sverre's work was a disaster.

His reputation as a wood-butcher preceded him, unfortunately, so that the kind of carpentry he got involved lots of ditch digging (he considered becoming "a sewer specialist") and only occasionally carpentry work involv-

Those little markings on a ruler threw him for a loop . . .

ing actual construction of something, this happening when the jobber didn't give doodly about the aesthetic results.

For example, if some local farmer wanted to add a shade-covering structure behind the pig-house, and didn't really care if the structure leaned a little to one side afterwards, Sverre was the man to build it. He came cheap, anyway.

These nothing-carpentry-jobs annoyed Sverre who dreamed of being a real carpenter with a real construction crew, and in a moment of irrational thinking, a local builder Bob Johnson hired him for a quick project that had to be completed in a big hurry.

This was the moment! Turned out to be hardly much more work than that, too, as Sverre was done as a carpenter that day (actually by noon; in the afternoon he was back to ditch-digging).

What got to Bob and fellow carpenters was at first amusing and then annoying as the men ended up having to redo Sverre's assignments themselves, unless, of course, they could mentally picture some tape measure and make some quick conversions.

When Sverre was sent to measure a door-frame so that Bob could cut a board for it, Sverre called back the following measurement after scrutinizing his yellow tape: "It's three feet, two inches, plus one big mark and one little mark." That was as close as he could come, close counting only in horse-shoes and grenade explosions.

Sverre's extraordinary words would get gleefully repeated in the taverns for weeks afterwards. Meanwhile, Sverre got a real job driving dump-truck for the county.

The Might and Myth
of a One-Day-Toot

Hjalmer Bjorn Ruspegaarden performed a miracle once a month. On himself. It was a bodily miracle of sorts in which Hjalmer went from an arthritic, bent, shuffling, snarling, whining, mean old man to a converted, snappy-looking, brisk-walking, stand-up-straight, smiling, gregarious personality happy with himself and in love with the whole world, or rather, "da 'hole, vide vorld, den."

An aging veteran of the First World War, bachelor Hjalmar Ruspegaarden lived with his sister, and at their home he mainly grumped and sat and sat some more on the wooden, front-porch swing-set, which variety could be found on every front porch in town. A front porch without a swing-chair was naked.

At his house he was always too tired — and ornery — to mow the lawn (their foot-high grass showed it) to take off the storm windows (theirs were the first storm windows to be up in the fall because they had never been taken down in the spring), to do any household chores ("vomen's vork," he sniffed).

Only with great effort could Hjalmar raise himself off the porch-seat with the aid of his ever-present, stout cane, and once he got his hulk raised up, he'd take tiny, mincing steps back into the house where he'd quickly go do again on a mohair divan and there take long naps, naps, he said, in honor of his hero, Calvin Coolidge, the greatest (napping) president of all time. The two had much in common, as judging by Hjalmar's disposition; he, like Coolidge, had been weaned on a dill pickle.

Persons walking by his dilapidated house would regularly see a collapsed Hjalmar sitting on the porch, sitting

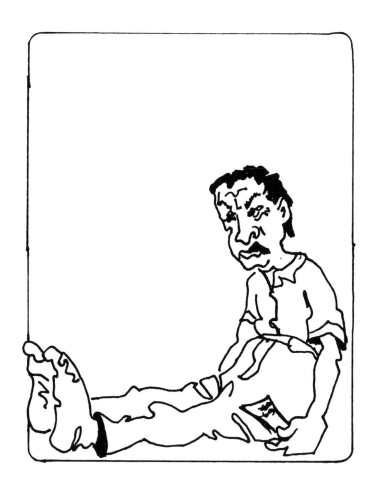

He, like Coolidge, had been weaned on a dill pickle . . .

there all scrunched down, an unsmiling Buddha, not responding to a single pleasant "Hello," and responding to any **"God dag"** (good day) with curled-lip sarcasm: "Whuz so damn gewd 'bout it?"

Phone callers asking him to go along fishing or picking berries or just taking a ride were offers curtly rejected. Hjalmar seemed always to want to sit and nap and sit some more before going back to the divan. In between he practiced his sneering. All this inactivity became a pattern, a ritual for an ornery old buzzard.

Yet both the ritual and the man changed one day each month, miracle-day, the day he got his veteran's pension check. Even that one day became a kind of ritual for the townspeople to observe and expect.

It started in the morning when the bank opened its doors. Housewives living along main street could look out the window and observe on the sidewalk this lean, lonely figure leaning heavily on a cane, the man bent half-way to the ground, and barely advancing forward at a snail's pace.

Every step Hjalmar made seemed to be done with great pain. The frightful frown on his rugged, lined, red face suggested there was not an ounce of happiness in that man. Everyone in town knew him, knew the situation, knew enough to leave him alone at that time, knew fully well also that he'd be coming back a changed figure.

When Hjalmar finally but finally eased himself into the bank and got his check cashed, the next and only remaining stop left was the tavern across the street. Crawling up on the barstool was almost an impossible task for him to accomplish, but once perched on top, Hjalmar's miracle began.

One schooner of brown beer followed another in rapid succession. In an hour, by the time he had to make his first of many trips to the lavatory — "gotta go see Missus Jones" — sufficient alcohol had chemically moved into his bloodstream and to the brain so that both body and soul had made turn-about alteration. Hjalmar got pickled.

By then he could crawl off and on the stool with ease

and speed. By then he could declare jovially that his kidneys had reached their saturation point because he was drinking what he called "World-War II beer." "Yup," said he with a big smile, "it's P-38 suds dey sell here, den. Ya da-rink vun an' ya pee t'irty-eight. Har har har."

By then he would regale his fellow tipplers with joke after joke, progressively enjoying each one better than the last. Sample: Didja hear havat dat Jewish guy said in Ja-roos-lem hven he found out how cold it iss in Minn-sota in da vinter? He sess: 'Aye t'ank yew, Lord, dat Yew din't send Moses dere!' Har har har."

By then he'd have lined up a fishing trip: "Ya-da, den, le's go to Sand Lake an git uss some of dem pound-**caruser** (blue gills)" — which trip he'd turn down the next day.

By the time Hjalmar was ready to go home, he felt no pain, no strain. Mellow and agile were the new words to be carried through. He'd hop down quickly from the stool, even do a little jig, and practically dance out the door, leaving all with a hearty good-by and a "**Ha det bra**" (Have a good time) — and invariably leaving his cane, too. (The sister would come in the next day to pick up the again-needed cane and at the same time she'd give the bartender a piece of her mind for "getting my dear brother inebriated.")

Returning up the same sidewalk, this time at a lively pace, and occasionally adding a skip or two, Hjalmar would stop to greet every person he met: "**God dag.** How she goin', den? Grrr-eat day, issn't it." If he ran into kids, he'd reach into his pocket and give them coins. "Youse kids lewk t'irsty, den., Here, go git some pop."

It was indeed a new and happy Hjalmar when he arrived home. But once inside it wasn't so happy as his sister had her say, angry words said with quantity and speed. ("Ya," said Hjalmar the next month, "dat sister can talk like da vind, 50 miles an hour, vit gusts up to a hunnert vords a minute.")

The next day and days, back to gloom and doom, to aches and anger, negativism and naps. But wait 'til the end of the month! "Gotta go see Missus Jones." Time to be "happy" and "healthy" — just one day in the month. The whole thing was pathetic, and everybody knew it except one person, Hjalmer Ruspegaarden.

Their get-up-and-go had got-up-and-went . . .

The Hired Man;
Historical . . . and gone

At one time in our history, notably those decades preceding World War II, a basic institutional figure associated with rural life in general and farming in particular was someone known simply as The Hired Man.

Almost every farm owner in our lutefisk ghetto had a hired man for at least a portion of the year, especially at haying and threshing time. Some farmers with big farms had year-around help, and it was these full-timers who should earn the true title of The Hired Man.

Nowadays, hired men are as scarce as hens' teeth on farms. In fact, nowadays even hens are scarce on farms. Time was, however, when The Hired Man and The Farm were two terms that went together as commonly as Homer and Jethro, a beer-and-a-bump, Model-A's and Makin' Out.

Historically and economically, The Hired Man is important; collectively, they were important; individually — based on my personal acquaintance with most of the hired men around our community — they all had in common primarily one thing: they drank too much.

What historians say of "the cowboy" is comparable to "the hired man." When observers strip away the veneer of romance, bravery, and daring-do associated with the cowboy, what they find is a figure of limited ambition and/or brains who, if the cowboy were to amount to something in that category, would become a cattleman. If the guy did not have the wherewithal to move up to Cattleman, he remained a cowboy, and that was a position rather low in the pecking order. In the same sense, if a hired man remained forever a hired man, well, it was a clear sign to most farmers that the guy didn't have it to become a Farmer. Importantly, at least the cowboy still has the aura of romance about him, even if it is fictitious. Who cares about economic or social truth? That's boring. So what if the standard cowboy may have been mentally deficient, morally lacking, and had the get-up-and-go of a drugged zombie, at least the American public perceives the cowboy as a hero! —even if it's all baloney. The myth of the cowboy lives on.

Perception is the reality; that's not baloney, and so they make movies and more movies and TV shows about cowboys. Has there ever been a single film, a single TV show about hired men on a farm? Would John Wayne ever have accepted such a role?

The only nationally semi-famous hired man is in Robert Frost's long narrative poem, "The Death of a Hired Man," and that particular death was little to mourn. The guy was a loser.

All the hired men that I ever knew were pretty much losers, too. They closely fit the definition of basic cowboys, namely low ratings in those categories that would be required to "make something of themselves," so that "they'd amount to something," old and familiar lines of assessment. Most of them had pilot-lights that burned a bit low, and their get-up-and-go had got-up-and-went. The somber truth about the hired man is forgotten. Small loss.

But maybe my bias on this topic comes from the fact that it was Soren Skogfjorden's hired man who shot my little dog when I was about ten years old, who killed my dog, or so he informed my inquiring father, "just for the hell of it," disgusting rationale I didn't understand then nor now.

Farmer Soren Skogfjorden, our neighbor, hired an ongoing array of peculiar men. It seemed that he alone hired more farm weirdos than all his neighbors together. Hired men came and left Soren's Guernsey-Dairy-Farm like revolving doors turning, leaving often by request, like when Soren's wife found missing pairs of her daughters' panties all hidden under the mattress in the bed where the hired man slept. That guy was spooky. Usually the men quit Soren when there were enough funds saved permitting them to go on a good, long toot. A curious sign of a hired man's "success" among his peers was the length of time one could stay on a drunk. A weekend? Pure nothing. A whole week? Pretty good. Two to three weeks? Marvelous! An entire month? Worthy of praise of the highest magnitude! A hero to emulate! King of the manure pile!

Finally, when the toot tootled out, maybe it was back to Soren's once again, hat-in-hand, full of promises and "I'll never do it again." Certainly Weslock Skurvik was a revolving-family-member for Soren for several years, coming and going as regular as the meter-reader. (In retrospect, Soren was as much a welfare worker as a farm owner. Workfare is an old concept.)

All the hired men in our area came to town on Sunday afternoons, their only time off all week, there to sit elbow to elbow at the local taverns and drink and commiserate and drink and play pool and drink and play the jukebox and drink some more. All strived to get "t.b.," — tavern bellies, the bigger the belly, the higher their image.

The hired men both acted alike and looked alike on Sunday afternoons. This meant a white,starched shirt, but no tie; a long-sleeved shirt with the cuffs rolled up to the elbows, but no higher. This meant dark, gabardine slacks with shiny rear ends, the pants held up with a leather belt, the holes punched with an eight-penny nail, and a beer-stomach hanging over the buckle like some extended porch. It meant black Oxford shoes and white cotton socks. It meant a pack of Lucky Strike or Camels cigarettes in the shirt pocket and farmers-stick-matches in the front pants pocket, matches lit by whipping the wooden stick along the thigh. It meant combed-back hair, hair parted and slicked back and shiny and smelly with Brilliantine or Vitalis. And it meant a billfold in the left rear pocket, a molded-to-the-rear leather container that held the week's wages, money to be blown on that one activity which seemed to be enjoyed far above any other, drinking.

Then came evening-chore-time on Sundays. As this bewitching hour neared, the majority would wobble out the tavern door and hobble back to their respective farmyards, there to semi-perform their expected barn duties, albeit a bit slowly.

But a tiny few hired men never moved off those barstools. They would be willing to risk it all with their host families and stay there in the tavern and really hang one on; none of this half-way stuff. They'd soak up the suds until poured out the front door at 1 a.m., then stumble towards their farms and sleep in the haymow, not knowing until the next bleary morning whether they were still hired men or not.

If it came out "not," well, then "T'ell wit'em," there were other farms, other jobs; they'd show 'em where the bear crapped in the buckwheat. There are lots of jobs. After all, farmers need hired men!

That was true in those years preceding advanced technology, but once machines got perfected allowing the farm owner to perform alone myriad jobs that once needed extra hands, the hired man was phased out as fast as he could say combines-and-milk-machines-and-ten-bottom-plows.

Hired men are almost all gone now. They fit in the ancient category along with buggy-whips, hand cranks, and kerosene stoves in summer kitchens. They're history now, and historically it would be important for an oral historian to try to interview former hired-men before they're all gone, just to get their stories on record. Yet there's a major problem even if there were 100 available historians to interview 1000 available hired men, and the problem is that they wouldn't likely talk. How can one interview mutes?

I personally recall hired men as being the least verbal figures in any occupation known. Except for those Sunday afternoon orgies when they'd open up enough and spill their guts on such controversial subjects as The

Weather, the men seemed as silent as Buddhist monks.

I never heard Johnny Larson's hired man, Walter Wrobleski, say ten words in ten years. Oscar Nottleson's man, Gilbert Hotvedt, seldom went beyond "Yups" and "Nopes" and if he were feeling loquacious that day, he'd add a "Maybe."

Was it the nature of the job? Some sense of silent honor to go along with silence-as-a-virtue? Well, the hired man for Nels Riistuben offered the opinion that anyone who strung more than five words together in one sentence was showing off, engaging in verbal diarrhea, and thus unworthy of either friendship or heaven.

Strong and silent were that peculiar breed, The Hired Man. Seeing that they're not likely to be interviewed in mass, perhaps a doctor should study the medical records of those who have passed on to "The Great Sunday Afternoon in the Sky" to determine the correlation between their passing and cirrhosis of the liver.

And maybe Soren Skogfjorden's cynical assessment might also be proven right: "When a guy becomes a hired man on a farm, his body undergoes a chemical change: "The iron in his blood turns to lead in his pants."

Shed one tear — and order one beer — for The Death, as it were, of the Hired Man.

The Loneliness of
A Holiday Hitch-Hiker

The tall, skinny hitchhiker had stood at that same spot beside the state highway for a long time, forever it seemed to him. Wrapped in an over-sized knee-length grey top-coat borrowed from his roommate, the coat may have had something going for it in fickle-fashion, but it was warmth that was needed at the time.

To be cold, and broke, and hitchhiking far from home at dusk is not an enviable combination. The coat collar was turned up high to offer limited protection from the bit-ter winter west wind. He wore no cap, no hat. Why? No self-respecting college student would wear a cap, even when it means freezing to death.

Only nerds wear warm caps, only nebishes dress to keep warm. At least the lonely hitchhiker believed he'd die in style there along the near-deserted highway as the fading December sun hung low on the horizon. Hands jammed down in the pockets, he danced back and forth from one numbed leg to the other, trying to keep the cir-culation going.

There was another kind of circulation going on in his mind, the notion that he wouldn't make it home that night, and that night happened to be Christmas Eve.

There is little to match the loneliness of someone who is away from home for the first time on Christmas Eve. Yes, there has to be a first time for everyone, of course, but that logic doesn't make it any easier at the time, especially when you're stranded and standing on frozen gravel and ice along some bleak highway.

It had been a long day. He had been traveling since sunrise and managed a series of rides that got him

To be cold and broke, and hitch-hiking far from home . . .

through two states already and now he was into the third and final state, but still 100 miles from home. He felt like it could have been 100 thousand miles, as either figure still meant his destination was far away. That distance between one traveling point to another is an interim. You're not really there until . . . well, until you're there.

His near-empty big suitcase sat beside him, the satchel containing only dirty laundry, but this suitcase — also borrowed — had a large initial on the side of it, a blue and white "L." It was important to convey the message to wary motorists that this suitcase owner was indeed some poor college kid trying to get home on the cheap.

The "L" had worked well all day long, with almost all drivers telling him that they wouldn't have picked him up if they hadn't figured he was a school boy.

But now it had stopped working. Worse, the sun was setting and it was getting dark, and no driver would pick up a stranger after dark even if the guy had ten suitcases with phosphorescent letters spelling "Hey, I'm o.k. I'm not a murderer!"

Getting more dejected by the minute, the young man's limbs were getting numb from the cold, so once again he ran across the road to his "savior," a gas station still open. In the last two hours it had become a pattern: stand there till you couldn't take it any more, then dash to the station, get thawed out, then tear out again the moment you spied an auto hurtling down the highway, raise that bony arm in a futile gesture as the cars whizzed by, the drivers not so much as glancing at the depressed kid about to miss his first Christmas Eve at home.

As darkness descended, the number of cars going by decreased dramatically; hardly any traffic was moving, but this was expected. On Christmas Eve people stay home and highways are nearly deserted.

Now more bad news, maybe disastrous news, from the gas station manager. The man was closing shop early and heading home: "Sorry, kid, ya gotta get outa here soon. Five more minutes I lock the door."

A glance out the soiled window showed a big semi-truck way down the road but heading towards him, and once again he grabbed his bag and sprinted across the highway in time to make the proper sign, but once again it hurtled past him. Through the flying snow he thought he saw the brake-lights flash on the truck, but naw, the rig disappeared around the sharp curve. Besides, truckers don't pick up hitchhikers anyway.

Back to the gas station for one final warming. And after that? He didn't want to think about it. The manager had the key in his hand and made the motion of it's-time-to-leave, but he did add another "Sorry, kid," as he turned the lock behind him. In the dark, the boy stood there on the icy steps not knowing what to do.

He looked up as out of the dark emerged this hulking figure coming towards him, a big burly man who resembled a large black bear. The man stopped, offered no pleasantries, just barked at him: "Hey, you that guy tryin' to hitch a ride?"

"Yeah. YES!"

"Well hurry up and get the lead out. My truck's sittin' down around the curve and I'm losin' time so get your ass in gear an' c'mon."

The kid had to run to keep up with the trucker's walk. They came around the curve in the road and there stood this wonderful sight, this big rig, the diesel motor purring loudly, the multiple lights blinking happily in the dark. To the hitchhiker it was the most beautiful sight and sound in the world.

When both riders got seated up in the high cab, the purr turned into a loud roar and stayed at that volume as they pounded down the highway. The noise made conversation difficult, but it was just as well as any attempts made to talk to the driver were answered by one-syllable grunts. In that noisy cab they rode in verbal silence.

What was the man's name? Even when he repeated it twice it was still unintelligible to the hitchhiker, and the trucker's manner was so brusque that he didn't want to risk a third try.

What was the trucking company's name? There was

nothing printed on the cab or cab sides. These questions hollered at the driver came out the same way as his name, and any discussion halted when the driver said, "Hey, kid, do me a favor. Shut up."

Two hours later it required a careful tap on the shoulder, some fancy sign language, and a shouted "I'm almost home" to indicate that the fast approaching town was the kid's destination. Getting that truck geared down and finally halted was no small undertaking, but finally the rig stood puffing on the side of the road and the young man got ready to get out.

The kid was so appreciative of what that trucker had done for him, he wanted to thank him like he'd never thanked anyone before. He also wanted to get the man's name and his address, too, to write him and his company later. Given the day, the timing, and the circumstances involved, it would be one of the most memorable kindnesses ever done to him.

The young man turned to the driver and began to form his words carefully, but the trucker cut him off in mid-sentence: "Hurry up, kid, crawl out. I ain't gonna sit here all day. Move it!"

The kid then moved down the ladder-like steps and stood on the frozen ground. As he turned to reach up to slam the over-sized door, he looked up to catch a smiling truck driver who said, "By the way, kid, Merry Christmas."

The door slammed and he was gone.

P.S. The forlorn — then ecstatically happy — hitchhiker was me, of course, returning to our lutefisk ghetto from Luther College in Decorah, Iowa. To this day I wonder who that truck driver was, and to this day that trucker's actions remain one of the most special acts of kindness that I've ever experienced.

The Mystery
of the Beauty Parlor

Mrs. Ervina Bergson had her hair done each week. Thursday night was her night to go to the beauty parlor, without fail. This trivial event went on year after year with no change.

Whatever the season, whatever the weather, whatever the month or year, Thursday night was the time Mrs. Bergson went to the beauty parlor, as hairstyling places were called in those years around World War II.

The above bland information telling of one plain housewife going off to have her hair fixed regularly could also be said of dozens of ladies in town who did the same thing each week, of course.

There was, however, a monumental difference between Mrs. Bergson and the other women, namely that Mrs. Bergson never went anywhere else. Never. Anywhere. Anytime. Anyplace.

She did not attend church, did not even go to the store to shop for groceries. Indeed, she would not step outside her house in the daylight hours. Mrs. Bergson was a genuine recluse.

There was doubt held by many townspeople that the strange Ervina Bergson actually had her hair done each week, but this assertion could easily be proven by standing in the shadows behind the beauty parlor any Thursday and there, after sundown, one could see a figure emerge out of the darkness and slip silently, unobtrusively through the back door.

Inside the beauty parlor, with all the venetian blinds drawn tightly, Mrs. Bergson became the only customer of the evening. The operator had no regular evening hours all week but did make this single, Thursday exception for Mrs. Bergson.

Thus, although a surprise to many, Mrs. Bergson did exist, even though hardly anyone in town ever saw her. The number of persons who actually viewed her in person could be counted on one hand, this over a period of nearly fifty years.

(I came close to it, once. Although I was a good friend of her son, only one single time — somewhere around eighth grade — was I inside their home, and even that semi-invite to come inside, but stay in the kitchen, was a spur of the moment decision as the son ran into change clothes quickly this one April afternoon before we went off after school to spear suckers and red-horses below the power dam.

(Inside the front door, the son called out those familiar two lines yelled by millions of kids coming home after school: "Hi, Mom, I'm home. What's there to eat?" A voice answered from another room, and, or so it sounded to me, a voice from another planet: "There's fresh-baked cookies on the counter and milk in the ice-box."

(Those were the only words I personally ever heard her say in my lifetime. Even then the mystery surrounding Mrs. Bergson was appreciated, even by us kids. Yet only once was her furtiveness ever hinted at by our gang to her son, and he simply tossed aside our curiosity with a shrug of nonchalance and a line of explanation to the effect that his mom just preferred to be alone. That was an understatement.)

The mystery of Mrs. Bergson would literally be carried to her grave. When she died, not a few of her nosy neighbors went to the funeral just to view the body. She fooled them again, however, as no one saw anything. Hers was a closed casket. Then the only thing that the townspeople could presume about her with some certainty was that her hair was fixed nicely.

Today I wonder the same exact thing that puzzled me about Mrs. Bergson almost a half century ago: Why did she have her hair fixed up nicely every week when she never went anywhere anyway?

Old Soldier
— or About Face!

There are some advantages in getting older. Maybe not too many, but yet there are a few. The term "older," of course, is a relative idea that means different ages to different people, depending on their own age.

Persons who are 65 regard 75 as "getting old," while on the other end of the scale, Americans under 30 regard 60 as "old-age"; and most teenagers, of course, regard anyone over 30 as also over the hill. To them, "getting old" is equated with getting leprosy.

Age was a major factor in our youthful perception of a retired man who moved to our community and lived literally only one year more. He had had a surprise marriage to a local widow, a woman of her husband's vintage, hence the surprise part. To us kids, any couple over age 50 who got married was mind-boggling and beyond comprehension.

We were junior high age at the time and we regarded this new stranger on the street as not only ancient but goofy. He always carried a brass-headed cane, for example, even if he didn't use it in walking. He wore white shoes amid a community where white shoes were expected to be worn only by female nurses in hospitals.

Yet the most significant of all things worn by this newcomer was a row of military medals pinned to his outside garment, whether shirt or coat. He wore them every day. It was rumored that he received those medals for his being in the U.S. Army in Cuba during the Spanish-American War.

Although no one was sure of the man's military rank at

anytime, he was quickly dubbed "The Colonel," but this particular title was less a remark of respect than a term of sarcasm, and among our pimply crew, a term of derision aimed at this old fool putting on the dog because of some ancient war that happened maybe about the time of the Peloponnesian War. Wasn't that in 1898 too?

To us callow youths the time-frame for the Spanish-American War approximated that of the American Revolution. To us The Colonel was probably in the same birthday-category as George Washington.

Kids can grow up for the strangest reason . . .

Instead of regarding the veteran as an honorable figure still so proud of his patriotism that he wore his dangling medals daily, we perceived him as an aged buffoon, likely senile, a white-haired weirdo who was deserving of mocking laughter.

So when we would meet him on the street, we'd yell "Hi-ya, Colonel," and he sometimes replied with a jolly wave of his arm, and sometimes, not, as apparently he didn't -or wouldn't - hear our young voices. Just as well he didn't catch the nuances intended in our mock greetings as there was not one ounce of respect in them. They might better be judged as catcalls.

Soon it was obvious that The Colonel was aging quickly and his health departing almost daily. His former military bearing, his stand-up-straight manner, and his once sprightly walking pace all changed perceptibly. It appeared that almost overnight he became stooped, and his walk became more of a shuffle. His once spiffy appearance gave way to spots of jam and jelly on his shirt front, and his former white shoes became dirty and grimy-looking.

The worst change for him came when he could no longer control his bladder, and often he'd wet his pants right there on the main street sidewalk. That may have been the most offensive change but in retrospect what was even worse was that we kids thought it was funny at the time.

"Hi-ya, Colonel," we'd holler at him from across the street, and because he couldn't hear, we'd add "How's the plumbing?" We began to make up slogans: "Join the Army and End Up Like 'The Colonel'." Ha ha ha. "Uncle Sam Wants You - To Change 'The Colonel's Diapers'." Yuk yuk yuk. "Old Soldiers Never Die, They Just Smell That Way." Yukel yukel yukel.

And then something happened. One of our gang was a shirt-tail relation of the Colonel's wife, and for reasons now forgotten, invited me along to the Colonel's house which at that moment was unoccupied as the couple had gone out shopping.

It was while we were roaming around their big house that we stepped inside the large living room and saw it, this huge, framed picture hanging above the fireplace. We moved quickly forward and gazed upward at this vastly enlarged photograph, and there we saw The Colonel mounted on a sleek horse. The man was in full-dress uniform, sitting there so straight, holding a riding crop, his stern face and steely eyes looking straight down at us, and the whole scene was magnificent!

The man in the picture was so handsome, so dashing, so totally hero-like that he seemed to belong in some Hollywood movie. His big muscles were so obvious in that picture that they practically bulged out through the starched, shiny khaki shirt. He was wearing knee-high leather riding boots that glistened from spit and polish, and also glistening in the picture were a row of medals on his chest, the same ones he wore out on our streets every day.

What a different figure we saw within that huge wooden frame. And that picture was worth a thousand words, words that even got to the two skinny junior high punks gazing up at what had suddenly and mysteriously become a wonderful man.

There was more, a sort of capstone to the visual message, in case the picture was insufficient to explain the man. In the bottom corner behind the glass was a small sheet of yellowing paper, a personal letter with some handwritten words stating the gratitude of the writer for the superb bravery in action shown, how indeed the entire cavalry unit had likely been saved by the quick-thinking heroics of The Colonel. The letter was signed by Theodore Roosevelt.

That visit, that picture, that message were all it took for junior highers to realize that The Colonel had been a member of the famed Roughriders, had ridden with Teddy Roosevelt and received a personal letter of thanks from him for his bravery! Wow!

After that picture-event, we didn't care if we saw egg-yolk lying with the strawberry jam in the creases of his shirts; we didn't pay any attention to scuffed shoes, and we didn't even care if he wet his pants. After what he was, who he was, what he'd done, the man could do any damn dumb thing he wanted to do and we didn't care. He was a genuine hero who deserved respect, kindness and help.

Suddenly the "Hi-ya, Colonel" came out entirely differently from young mouths. Kids offered to help him across the street or run errands for him. There was a genuine warmth and affection in our eyes when we came up to him just to touch his arm and say our smiling hellos with a depth of new appreciation for a deserving senior citizen.

It was a complete about-face for a person who heretofore was regarded as a decrepit, loony old poop who we hoped was ready to kick the bucket by Wednesday, any convenient Wednesday.

It's amazing the power of photographs; it's also amazing how kids can grow up for the strangest reasons.

When Community Fairs Featured Old-Fashioned Oratory

Community fairs and political speeches used to go hand in glove together. There was a time when Fair supervisors in neighboring counties competed with each other as to which Fair could attract the biggest politician to come and give a real stem-winding talk to a large, fascinated, and appreciative audience.

Old-time political oratory was once very popular. Large crowds assembled at county fairs — there to sit on make-shift benches, camp stools, or on the hard ground — just to listen to a political speech that was expected to last at least an hour. Anything short of that amount of time was considered a gyp.

Audiences once expected quantity if not quality from their elected figures. Shades of William Jennings Bryan and the late Hubert Humphrey, two of the best public speakers of all time.

Political oratory used to be an art-form. Today it's a bore. Politicians nowadays are in minimal demand to even appear, let alone give long-winded speeches. They're hardly wanted at county fairs anymore — or anywhere else.

If political aspirants do happen to weasel their way to a platform and a microphone, they better cut off their words in twenty minutes or there'll be no one out there listening at the end.

Old-fashioned speeches are no longer wanted. Worse, they're ignored, with crowds staying away in droves. A U.S. Senator can announce that he will be giving a major address in some big-city auditorium and the tickets to be sold to voters who actually want to listen to him in person result in sales that might fill up the first two rows of chairs.

In sad contrast, if in the morning it was announced that the same big-city auditorium will be bringing Bruce Springsteen or Prince or Madonna, all the tickets will be sold out by noon.

These days, in order for politicians to get before the public, in person, they have to sneak their way into something already planned, like local parades, where people on the sidewalk have to look at them ride by and watch them give their oily smiles and their politicians' studied wave-of-the-arms.

In parades politicians wage losing battles with the area high school bands and majorettes whom the people came out to see in the first place. People grin and bear it for the politician — and quickly look down the street for the next float. "The poor politician ain't appreciated no more."

It wasn't always that way, as suggested, for politicians in general and notable statesmen in particular. Statesmen — defined by the cynics as "politicians who are very dead" — who could deliver fiery speeches, were once in great demand, providing they had name-recognition. No name? No stay. When a "nobody politician" got introduced at the local fairs, that was the signal for the crowd to get up and go see the blue-ribboned critters in the pavilions.

Such was the situation in our lutefisk ghetto when the big news was announced that the governor of the state, Walter Kohler, would be the featured speaker at the Fair on Sunday afternoon, the "prime time" of the entire three-day Fair.

Gov. Kohler was big news because his name was big news. Talk about name recognition! Just one glance down at the bathroom plumbing reminded people of their governor's name. Kohler of Kohler was a household word.

Fair supervisors also announced that a "nobody politician" would give an address following the governor's, this person picked to suggest bi-partisanship on the part of the supervisors. A Democrat and a Republican — but no party more radical than that — was accepted and ex pected. (A Socialist would have been run out of town, a Communist tarred and feathered. These "isms" can be carried too far!)

Come Sunday afternoon of the big Fair day, the area around the outdoor speaker's stand was jammed with citizens of all ages, many of them giving up the baseball game going on over at the ball field at the same time. People simply wanted to see their governor and most likely their future United States Senator. When baseball loses out to politics, then one knows there's an important man around.

The local Lutheran minister had been chosen to introduce the governor and the pastor was both long-winded and effusive of praise in his introductory remarks. Then followed the governor's hour-long address which was filled with caustic references and partisan humor aimed at his opposing party and that "nobody politician" who was waiting, servant-like, in the wings to follow him. A second-class citizen.

When the Gov. finished, everybody but everybody got up to leave, knowing full well that there was this other eager young man just waiting to get his chance at the mike. The crowd was not about to stay.

With the crowd already moving out and away, the introduction of "nobody" was hurriedly done so that he could start immediately and try to get some of the people back before they got out of sight and sound. The poor fellow at first pleaded with people to hear him out, to give him a chance, to listen to an alternative point of view.

It was useless. It was also pathetic. Despite the anguished pleas, people just turned their backs on him and continued to walk away, a few giving the wave of a disgusted good-bye to him and his ilk. They kept right on heading to the eat stands, the midway, and the beer pavilion. First things first.

A tiny few of us did turn around and went back and sat down. I stayed because very simply I felt sorry for the guy. The entire "crowd" to hear this second politician could have all gotten into a phone booth.

Today I do not recall a single word of his remarks. I recall only his manner, his sincerity, his believability, his integrity, the latter two items being a bit rare in that particular profession. He finished his comments in fifteen minutes and then thanked his handful of listeners profusely for "giving him a listen," as he phrased it, and came down to shake everyone's hand.

Since that day there have been perhaps millions of people who have given that same man "a listen." His name was and is William Proxmire, U.S. Senator from Wisconsin, who keeps getting re-elected over and over by wider margins each term over the past twenty-five years.

Governor Kohler in turn would quickly fade from the political scene, notably after his eventual loss to Proxmire. It is certainly a curious turn-about from that day when one community literally turned their back on Kohler's opponent.

There is an obvious moral here for all "nobodys" in politics or any other field: never give up.

Will the day ever return when political speeches are the highlight of county fairs? Yes, that will be the same day that pigs wear lipstick and the fair beer stands get closed down by the W.C.T.U.

GUINDON

Migrant lutefisk harvesters arriving for season.

You Know You're in a Small Town . . . When Louie Gets There First

A basic given fact in small town living is that everybody knows everybody. And everybody knows that everybody knows. That particular acceptance of village life has an extension to it, revealing an intimacy among community inhabitants that even goes beyond people, as this true account illustrates:

Mrs. Mabel Tollerud drove to town early, about 7:30, so that only the hardware store was open, a fact she knew well as she planned to buy her paint and start her project at home by 8 o'clock.

It was while Mabel was parking her sagging Chevy that she looked up and saw him. Then she immediately froze. "O M'Gawd!" she whispered out loud, "Louie's in town!"

Only when Louie had moved around the corner and headed down the hardware store alley and out of sight did she dare get out of the car. Forgetting about any paint for the moment, she made a bee-line for the telephone office, first to alert Daisy, the telephone operator on duty, and then to call her daughter at home.

"Daisy!" said Mabel, omitting any greetings or pleasantries, "Louie's in town! I gotta call home and warn Kari."

"Louie's downtown already? **Herre Gud**! (Holy God)" responded Daisy. "That means trouble. Just a minute and I'll get you through to home . . . but I see right now your party-line is busy. Want me to break in? It's just Klara Kolrue and Helena Wolden visiting about canning pickles this afternoon."

"Nah, let 'em finish. But as soon as it's free, call Kari about Louie. She's planning to ride her bike to town in an hour. This way she'll come alone, or she might not want to come at all."

"All right, then," agreed Daisy, who then thought to add: "I better notify Rena Kirkeby, too, as she shops early and always brings that monster of hers along wherever she goes." Daisy then hesitated before smiling perversely and thinking out loud: "Maybe we should let Louie show that monster a thing or two."

"Heavens! No! Daisy, how can you say such a thing like that? Well, I'll run to the grocery store now and tell'em there that Louie's in town, and then Karl can warn people who he knows shop this morning. Goodbye, then."

Mabel Tollerud walked to the door but hesitated before stepping out into the street. She knew that if she saw Louie, she'd stay right there where she'd be safe with the door closed tight.

Multiple glances in both directions indicated the coast was clear. Mabel then ran across the street, lickety-split, to Karl Jorgen's grocery store and she pounded on the locked door. Fat Karl inside heard the commotion and waddled forward to open up, then said: "It's a little early, but c'mon in anyway, Mrs. Tollerud."

"Karl, I don't want anything right now, I just came by to let you know that Louie's in town 'cause I know you'd want to know."

"That damn Louie," replied Karl, "He's a trouble-maker. Likely the worst one we got in town," mused Karl, who then thought to commend Mabel for her civic concern and early-warning system. "It's a good thing you told me. I'll call the constable and maybe he can get here in time and head off any more fights. Jeeez! That one last month was a doosy. Louie about killed Fritz, and I thought Fritz was pretty tough!"

"Fritz is no match for Louie anytime. I wish that Louie would try to pick on Frieda. My husband, he says that Frieda would show Louie who's boss, he says," replied Mabel, who added: " 'Course the real thing to do is to go to Louie's home and tell Melvin. That Melvin Grenlie lets Louie run around town like the wild animal he is!"

"Louie seems beyond control, all right. He runs away from the house all the time. He's really bad. A bad seed. If he were mine, I'd consider having him done away with. He's a menace to the community!" declared Karl.

At that moment Mabel looked around and there she spied Louie running down the sidewalk towards them. "HELP! Lemme inside!" screamed Mabel, who pushed her way past Karl just before the door got slammed behind her. Safely inside, both breathed a sigh of relief.

Then and only then did they both put their heads against the window pane in time to see Louie trot past the store.

Louie was a dog, the biggest, meanest, most vicious dog in town. Louie was part bulldog. Fat and ugly, Louie cleaned up on every dog who even dared come near him, hence the need for all the warnings to people who might be planning to bring their dogs to town that morning.

Only in small town can one inhabitant inform another inhabitant and convey total meaning to the vicissitudes of life by uttering one short statement: "Louie's in town."

Filling the Village Icehouse; Ah, When Men Were Men!(?)

The curious event happened each January. Its audience attraction had been usually limited to stray dogs, the village idiot, and one bored and nosy neighbor who lived on the same lakeshore but down a quarter of a mile from the action.

In later years, however, this event would attract more and more persons who came to the lake on the edge of town to witness — and shudder at — its grand finale, an episode that caused all the amazed viewers to question the sanity of the young fool involved.

This January ritual was the annual ice-cutting-and-storage procedure performed on a Sunday afternoon by the crew of Pete Peterson, a local dairy farmer whose economic sidelines included his being the town's ice-man, making home deliveries twice a week of block-ice hauled door to door in his ancient Studebaker pick-up.

A January Sunday was the day chosen because then Pete could hire a small crew wanting to pick up a few extra bucks from their regular week-day jobs. And January was the coldest month, of course, when the ice was the thickest and Pete could be assured of at least thirty-inch-thick blocks.

Cutting ice from lakes or ponds and hoisting these huge blocks up the long inclined wooden chute and into tar-paper-covered ice-houses was at least a special skill and sometimes an art-form. Certainly ice-storage was once a part of every community's winter projects in those days before refrigeration became common. Its carry-over today can be heard in the common terminology still used by older people who regularly refer to their refrigerator as "the ice-box."

Both special ice-cutting skills and certain ice tools were used in the process, starting with a Model-A Ford motor whose transmission had been hooked up to a large circular saw-blade. The removed engine had been mounted on skis and was tugged and pushed into place, the engine then started via many turns of the crank in front.

Once the machine was in the ready-position for cutting, the motor was revved up into high throttle and the spinning saw then lowered onto the blue ice beneath, the cutting producing a long white stream of snow and ice as the blade drove deeper through the hard crystals towards the water below.

Cutting straight lines some fifty yards long was difficult; cutting more straight lines to make each row the same width was even harder. Then criss-crossing those lines to resemble an ice checkerboard required high skills. It was dangerous, too, in that cutting too deep in the wrong place could send both man and machine to the bottom of the lake.

With practice over many years, Pete's crew would soon work that first-cut block into the end of the steep chute coming down from the ice-house and into the lake, at which point a two-inch hemp rope encircled the block and began to pull it slowly up the glazed planks and into the house by means of a homemade, handcrafted pulley-device powered by a single horse which made the same trip back and forth over and over again all afternoon.

The lake area in front of the chute gradually turned into a small pond as one by one the closest chunks were cut and pushed and pulled by long pike-poles into the chute opening leading to the clunking climb upwards.

Inside the icehouse to greet each sliding chunk were two strong men with heavy ice-tongs and the men would snare each block and with a combination of sliding, shoving and lifting, get the block in place and cover it with sawdust. Then little by little the crew filled up the gloomy structure one tier of ice at a time so that by late afternoon their heads would be touching the roof.

For most citizens in town, the event was so common

and humdrum — and cold — that they stayed away from the operation in droves. But this apathy changed primarily because of one Soren Buxengaard, a young man on the ice crew of great physical strength, if perhaps somewhat lacking in common sense.

Soren had chosen a dramatic way to end the day's work and the success of storing up enough ice to get his fellow townspeople through another hot summer. He chose to celebrate the occasion by jumping in the lake and going for a swim. A one-man Polar Bear Club.

The timing of the crowd to see Soren's leap into madness was such that most people waited until the sun was low before bundling up in scarves and leather choppers and thick stocking caps to witness that goofy Soren Buxengaard dive in.

Soren never disappointed his fans when that right moment came for his performance. With the Model-A engine shut off, the horse unhitched from the whiffletree, the wooden chute pulled out of the water and lying on shore, with the job indeed done, that's when Soren would begin his ritual, starting with stripping his clothes in front of everyone. Gypsy Rose Buxengaard, the stripper.

Off came the woolen coat, off came the 12-inch leather boots and home-made knit woolen stockings, off came the bib overalls and the flannel shirt, and off came the required second pair of wool pants, until at last Soren stood there barefooted on the ice wearing only his swimming "trunks," a one-piece union suit of white, woolen long underwear; "long-johns" they were called.

For this particular moment the school kids skating on the lake in the shoveled-off area had tripped their way through the deep snow to come over and stand by the water's edge, the black water pushing up steam which ominously rose into the frigid air.

For this moment it seemed that half the town was there encircling the entire open water, standing there shivering, shifting from one leg to another to try to stay warm, and shifting spots too, to better see Soren and waiting impatiently for Soren to "do it" quick so they could hurry home to stoke up their wood stoves again before turning on "The Shadow" radio program. Hurry up, Buxengaard! Do it!

With plenty of yelps and hoo-hoos of crowd support — "That-a-way, Soren!" — and the old men saying quietly to each other: **"Han er galen"** (He's nuts) — Soren would dance about along the water's edge, then run back about twenty feet, eye the forbidding water, holler "Here goes nothin'!," sprint as fast as he could towards the threatening opening, and cannon-ball in, making a big enough splash, hoping to wet those timid souls nearest him.

Soren's head would bob up above the water and then would come his line, "Feels great!" — an assertion that seemed questionable to the awed onlookers. Then he'd swim back to the ice edge on his back, all the time blowing out water like a tiny white whale.

Quickly he'd haul himself back on the ice and more quickly wiggle himself back into his clothes again as the crowd broke with heads shaking and murmurs of county-asylum-inmates increasing by one.

Ice-cutting-and-storage was over again for another year.

Leftover . . .
Lutefisk Ghettoes

Teaching School
Amid Scandinavians

There are still Lutefisk Ghettoes to be found all over the Middle West. These pockets of primarily Scandinavians pop up regularly along the highways, but it's along the bi-ways where even stronger ethnic carry-overs remain.

If remote from major inter-state routes, it is easier for out-of-the way towns to retain their heritage as they do not have all those "foreigners" coming in all the time to alter the old ways.

Retained old world customs are all a matter of degree, of course. To hear a Scandinavian language spoken on the streets currently is unusual, whereas two generations back it was common. And yet one can still hear Norwegian spoken on the street corners today in towns like Spring Grove and Roseau, Minnesota; in Hatton and Portland, North Dakota; in Decorah and Roland, Iowa; in Iola and Osseo, Wisconsin, even if it is mainly old-timers who **snakker Norsk** (talk Norwegian).

It is this last town mentioned, Osseo, Lutefisk Ghetto II, where I got my first real job — a public school teacher of history and English (at the munificent starting salary of $3,200.00 a year).

There are wags who maintain that first-year teachers should pay the local school board, rather than vice versa, considering all that the beginning teacher learns that first term. There may be some perverse merit in that logic, but it does not pay the teacher's rent.

Certainly it was a great learning experience (alas, I learned more than the kids did) teaching five separate classes of some 150 students, but the job involved far more functions and duties never imagined at the start. These extras were assigned by the principal as part of the language agreement in the contract whereby the teacher agreed to accept "such other duties as may be assigned." That was all the legalese necessary for my assignments: sophomore class advisor, senior-commencement-advisor, school annual and newspaper advisor, forensics and speech coach, director three one-act plays, director of one three-act play, assistant basketball coach, and head baseball coach. Not be forgotten are ticket-seller, and chaperoning events from school proms to bus-rides to out-of-town games. For all these extra duties not one red penny extra compensation was paid.

Well, when you're a brand new teacher, you don't know any better. When the principal barked "Jump," that was not the time to bring up "teacher rights," it was the time to answer "How high?" However, given the amounts of both teaching and extra-curricular duties, I did think even then that the principal could also tie a broom to my rear end so that I could sweep the floors at the same time that I ran up and down the halls.

Only the most naive people believe that public school teachers teach only their favorite subject matter in neat, attractive, well furnished classrooms where thirty clean, attractive children sit attentively, patiently and courteously, eagerly soaking up every morsel of information, grasping every pearl of wisdom dropped from the instructor's lips. Sorry, it ain't like that. It's more like, well, being a lion-tamer at a decrepit zoo where the animals not only resist learning but defy instructions and instructors: "Down, DOWN you varmints! Get back, BACK in your chairs!"

During my first month of teaching at this zoo, I was absolutely petrified with fear before getting to school each morning. Along my walking route was this large bush where I could hide behind briefly and vomit from nervousness. Before too long, this sickness was happening so regularly that all I had to do was see the bush and the results came immediately. I changed my walking routine.

In retrospect, however, what is remembered the most

about that first teaching job are the kids themselves, the primary subject in this section, reporting both on 1) what happened then, and also 2) where they are now a third of a century later, if known.

It is these true accounts, mainly with students (with names altered) — along with related people and events — that follows. In all cases where the word "teacher" is mentioned, it is myself being referred to, this form adopted because of a stubborn Norwegian's reluctance to use the first person pronoun. (At least it's an improvement over columnists who use the imperial "we" when they really mean simply "I.")

Dora Hukebo

Sixteen-year-old Dora Hukebo sat in the first row, there on the end chair where she spent her time gazing out the window and paying not the slightest attention to what was going on in class.

Dora's recent inattention had been a change because she had started out to be a very good student, one who listened carefully and later took a lively part in class discussions.

The young, skinny teacher had watched her daydream for a full week straight. She maintained those glazed eyes during what he thought were outstanding presentations he had worked out on Jacksonian Democracy. Trouble was coming.

Finally by Friday he'd had it with Dora, she with the far-gone vacant expression on her ace indicating clearly that her mind was a long way from either the classroom or Andrew Jackson.

Anyway, this particular Friday the teacher chewed her out in front of the whole class for daydreaming. He said nasty, sarcastic things, and then threatened to kick her out all together if she didn't shape up. "Shape up or ship out," were his final words.

During his blistering remarks the rest of the class members sat there silently and sullenly. Dora began to cry. Everyone there understood the situation - except the dumb teacher.

After the class period ended, two of Dora's good friends hung around and when it was just the three of them, the friends informed the huffy teacher that Dora was . . . ah, . . . well . . . very pregnant.

The teacher was very shocked. And then very ashamed of his unnecessary cruel comments stated to assuage a touchy ego. He remembered a warning about teaching. "All teaching is done under conditions of stress, almost all of which the teacher is not aware of." No one in that room had the extreme stress as that of Dora Hukebo; it's little wonder that she had not interest in Jacksonian Democracy.

(Dora would soon marry the young father, her classmate, and after a few rough years, they would end up moving to California.)

Everyone understood . . . except the dumb teacher . . .

Willie Olson

Willie Olson was not a bad kid. The new teacher only thought he was a bad kid. Willie was tuned into a different channel, and Willie sort of did what he wanted to do, but the teacher wanted Willie to do only what he was told to do. Willie balked; the teacher bucked. Confrontation time.

After class he got Willie alone, went up to him nose to nose and said in a very loud, threatening voice: "You shape up, Willie, or I'll pound your head right through that brick wall!"

Willie Olson was six feet, four inches tall and 220 pounds of solid muscle. He was a top linebacker on the football team and could do one-hundred pushups — with one arm!

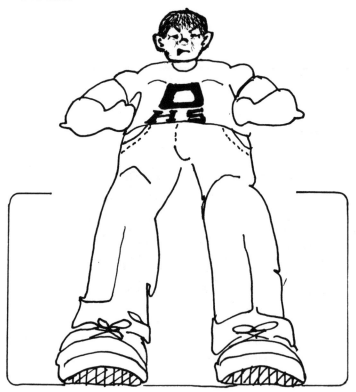

Y'know, teach, you're gonna get yourself killed someday . . .

The new teacher was six feet tall and weighed one-hundred and thirty nine pounds. Ichabod Crane had nothing on him in physique.

After the vocal charge, Willie looked down at this strange creature-teacher, smiled, shook his head in disbelief, then turned around and walked away. He turned back at the door and said quietly: "Y'know, Teach, you're gonna get yourself killed someday if you keep saying dumb things like that to the wrong guy. Y'know?"

(Y'know, Willie was right. Wow! Was he ever right! There are many morals to be gained from the above incident, the most obvious being: Never make threats; you might have to carry them out. Another coincidental lesson is the point that teachers should primarily discipline on a one-on-one situation. Willie may not have acted or answered so generously had there been a circle of his friends around to hear that dumb threat. Uff da, one shudders to think of what might have happened. Willie is a farmer and a trucker today and presumably he has the same good sense as the day he saved his teacher from his own stupidity.)

Darold Oldenberg

He raised his hand excitedly just after roll was taken, and he then said very seriously:

"It's important we take class time so I can tell you what happened to me this weekend. Wow! Was that somethin'! I thought I was a gonner for sure," he added, and before the teacher could head him off, Darold was rattling on with his tale of kidnapping:

"When I hitchhiked home after school on Friday, these two skuzzy-looking nerds in this beat-up truck picked me up and they wouldn't let me out when we got to our road, and Man-O-Man, was I scared! They had guns, too! These wackos drove down this old side road and drove into this abandoned farm and they dragged me inside this haunted house and pushed me into this empty room and locked the door behind me. I figures they were a couple of sex-maniacs for sure. Really! Then I discovered that one window wasn't nailed shut and I sneaked over there and quiet-like opened it and began to crawl out, but just then they rushed into the room and grabbed me by the leg and I was halfway out the window to safety, but they hung on and kept pulling and pulling, and kept pulling, too, and it was just awful! I thought my body would get pulled into two pieces but they kept pulling and I kept pulling my leg — just the way I've been pulling your leg for the last five minutes. Ha ha ha ha ha ha!"

(The teacher should have known better, having been bested before — and many times afterward — by Darold, still one of the funnest and funniest students I've had in over thirty years of teaching. He would become a plumber and would move to Tucson, Arizona, where likely he's still pulling legs as well as pipes.)

Kari Swenson

Kari fit the image of every teacher's dream of what all high school kids should be like. She was a gem, a jewel, a superior academic student, and just a wonderful kid.

But she was hardly "a kid," showing more maturity and common sense than many of her teachers. Tall, lean, nice looking, too, she was a joy to have around and to be around. She excelled with ease in everything curricular and extra-curricular, with one exception, that area in which she wanted to excel the most: public speaking.

The problem: Kari Swenson had the worst/best Norwegian accent ever deemed possible in a late 20th century public school student. She said lines like: "Aye wuss in town tewday." And "Yeah, dat wuss trew-ley pussling, den," and after any line showing doubt, she would wrinkle her pug, Scandinavian nose. Curiously — miraculously? — this was the same senior girl who won an A-rating at the state speech tournament held at the University. She did a superior job in the difficult category of Extemporaneous Speaking. Perhaps her success can

Kari Swenson had the worst/best Norwegian accent . . .

be explained in the amazing and amusing comments of the judge following her performance in the final round: "Your English is remarkably good for being a foreign student."

(Kari would go on to graduate from the state university. Today she lives in up-state New York with her engineer husband. They have four children and their heritage can be viewed by noting their names: Bjorn, Solveig, Eric, and Margit.)

Arvid and Arne Pederson

Arvid and his brother Arne were both high school juniors, this rank obtained by the grace of D-minuses throughout their school careers.

The bigger brother was called Pete, the smaller one named Re-Pete, the latter an appropriate designation for the number of classes retaken.

Farm boys, both, but they were not like most of the farm kids in that neither Pete nor Re-Pete changed clothes or washed after doing their farm chores before coming to school.

The brothers smelled badly of the contents of the stable. Other students shunned them, unless they had bad colds, because they both stunk to high heaven! Unfortunately, that dubious honor was the only "recognition" they received from their peers — except for this one day, the only day in their high school careers when they were singled out by their classmates for praise!

Honor-Day for the Pederson boys came that day that the American history student projects were due. All students were required to make something, anything "historical," but they had to do it with their own grubby fingers. No Lincoln Logs, no tinker-toy building, no kits to assemble. This assigned project led to too many Betsy Ross flags and an abundance of soap-carvings of George, Abraham, and Theodore, but it took Pete and Re-Pete in their joint-project to show everyone how quality work could be done, even if for a dumb history class that they hated — and found about as relevant to their daily lives as studying Swahili Gutteral.

On D-Day — "Projects Due Day" — the Pederson boys came carrying into the school from the back of their pickup a heavy ten by six foot plywood board, on top of which they had built an entire farmstead in miniature. The boys had everything there from barn to henhouse to wind-mill, from hayfield to corn shocks to outhouse. Even more, even better, underneath the thick board they had a series of little motors attached through holes cut in the plywood to the farm-scene items above. Hence the wind-mill turned, the horses moved, the farmer chopped wood with an ax. The whole thing was absolutely superb!

Everyone who saw the Pederson boys' work knew it was superb, all except Pete and Re-Pete, who couldn't understand all the fuss being made. All the students' efforts/models — some absolutely lugubrious, so bad that even a mother would be ashamed of her kid's incompetence — were placed on a series of tables in the general hallway. Primarily because of the farm scene, all grades K-12 were let out to see the displays, come and see this magnificent history project built by two of the big-gest screw-offs and general history haters in the entire high school.

For just this one day the other kids were slapping Pete and Re-Pete on the back amid shouts of praises: "Jeeeez! Hey, that's really GREAT! Really somethin', Y'know?"

But they didn't "y'know." The Pederson brothers did not know how to react to compliments, having never received any before. Each had the social grace and general respon-sive vocabulary of a stump, and so the boys stood there in bewilderment, making inarticulate gutteral sounds and cackled nervous laughter.

And yet amid this bewilderment on their part, each brother was so obviously pleased and proud of what they had made that the teacher wanted to grab them and hug them both — after first taking a long, deep breath.

When the "exhibition" ended, the brothers had raised

their history report cards to a shining C-minus, their highest academic award to date. After that they immediately returned to their old habits, old ways, old attitudes, and both would quit school — "The JAIL" — the day they hit age sixteen.

(I haven't the foggiest notion of whatever happened to the Pedersons. I suspect that today they still don't give a hoot in a rain barrel for education in general and history in particular, but I still hope that they can still remember with deserved pride that one day in their formal schooling when they shone so brightly and so deservedly because of their marvelous history project.)

Once he started to snore . . .

Eldred Mork

The new teacher did not know his students well, nor their families, nor the town in general. But he would learn.

Day after day Eldred Mork would come late to his first period class. This high school sophomore always had that signed tardy slip required of and from the principal, so apparently there was not problem with Eldred's tardiness in the head office.

That same tardiness annoyed the teacher. Why should this slovenly kid be late almost every morning? Is that any way to learn good job habits for the future? What an undependable, good-for-nothin' brat!

Not only was Eldred late, he'd sometimes fall asleep when he got there. Not just in a daydreaming state, but conked out sound asleep. Once he started to snore.

All the other students in class seemed to accept Eldred's tired manner as normal, but the new teacher didn't like it one bit. He found it insulting that any student of his would be so gauche as to put his head down on the arm of the desk and nap right in front of him. That was an affront! Eldred was a loser, a real loser.

So this one day when Eldred began sawing wood, the teacher let him have it. He woke him abruptly, then denounced him thoroughly in front of everybody and concluded his negative remarks by ordering the kid to get out of there and go down to the principal's office! Eldred just shrugged, yawned, and ambled out the door.

Less than a minute later the principal stood in the doorway and beckoned the teacher to come out in the hall. Said the principal very quietly:

"I think you should know that Eldred is the oldest of five children and is really raising the family himself. His father deserted years ago. His mother is the town tramp who too often does not bother to come home at night. It's a rough home-life there and Eldred takes up the slack. Last night he was up all night nursing a kindergarten-age sister with the flu. He never got to bed himself. About six a.m. he gets the rest of his brothers and sisters up, gets them washed and dressed and feeds them breakfast, and then off to school. That situation happens too often, and that's why he's often tardy himself. Just thought you'd want to know."

(The teacher did want to know, did eat humble pie, too, and afterwards let Eldred rest any time he wanted to. Eldred would end up a career-Navy man.)

Emil Egli

The Norwegianness of the community was strong enough so that the principal considered adding a Norwegian language class to the curriculum. French, German, Spanish? Heck, any school could offer them! What would really be special was Norwegian. It was special, all right, more special than the principal wanted.

Before adopting and adding this new class, the principal believed that a "preliminary experience" had to be tried first. Turned out that this test-run ruined any immediate future attempts, and yet the disaster was all so innocent!

The principal brought to the school for one hours a young man from Norway who wanted to become an American and a school teacher here. His name was Emil Egli and young Mr. Egli obviously knew Norwegian well but he did not know street-language English well; that lapse doomed the study of Norsk.

Mr. Egli began the experimental class with about thirty volunteers. He started with the basics, the A-B-C's, and that went fine at first as he would pronounce the letter and follow it with a word illustration of the same sound. Then the class members would say the Norwegian word together.

It was when he got to the letter F that his teaching began to come apart. The Norwegian word he chose for F was "fart," a word meaning speed or quickness, and it's a common word and term — in Norway.

To a bunch of American high school kids, however, the same word was immediately received with shock and surprise, then giggles and snorts and suppressed guffaws, reactions that made the unknowing Mr. Egli stubbornly curious about this suddenly strange student behavior before him.

He didn't have the sense to simply drop the matter and go on to the letter G. Instead, he insisted that the entire class say "fart" in unison, loudly and clearly. Instead of volume, he got only more titters and laughs — and red faces on the girls while the boys could hardly contain themselves.

They all verily yelled at the top of their lungs, 'FART'...

"Hvat's da matter wit yew?" he asked, a bit testily. "Aye vant yew all ta say togedder now, good and loud, 'FART!'" This encouragement convinced the back-row boys to really get caught up and swing with it, so they all verily yelled at the top of their lungs, "FART FART FART!" And then they broke up, one of the kids falling on the floor and holding his stomach.

In confusion and anger, Mr. Egli returned to his native tongue and yelled **"HOLD KJEFT!"** (Be quiet), but the kids didn't understand him and likely at that point wouldn't have paid any attention to him anyway.

Poor Mr. Egli didn't know what had happened or what to do. He did know that he was not being treated very courteously, so he scooped up his books and paper and walked out the door in a huff.

So ended Norwegian in this public school curriculum.

Ivadelle Paulson

The ongoing hassling among class members went on regularly as the students moved between periods from class to class - before finally settling down to begin the new period. The jeers, cat-calls, occasional swats and general harassment became part of each day's expected sophomore and sophomoric behavior, with little of the action taken seriously by either students or teachers.

Most of the general teasing was not deeply meant or felt. It just seemed a natural stage in how kids grew up, how kids interact with each other in their weird ways and all in all as American as . . . well, as public school students' behavior.

Sure, some kids seemed to catch a little more of the barbs than others, like Ivadelle Paulson, a fat farm girl, kind of a loner, who forever seemed to be swatting off attacks on her both verbal and physical. But any attacker paid for the attack!

Ivadelle was good at reacting. When some greasy-haired boy would poke her on the shoulder and holler, "Hey, Iva-in-the-Dell, I ain't seen that much fat since Pa butchered a pig," Ivadelle would snap back, "Try poking your own belly, Lardo. Geez, whata nerd! When God gave out brains, you thought he said trains, and asked for a long one."

Ivadelle seemed to handle herself well in these ongoing attacks, but it was clear that the kids liked to pick on her more than anyone else. Yet she'd come back with snappy lines and maybe a swing of the arm too, because she was feisty and could fight back. In these almost daily confrontations with Ivadelle, most of the kids watching would laugh,and the teacher sometimes laughed too, and did nothing to stop the teasing or defend her.

Then one morning as the class members came noisily careening into the room, the brashest boy of all said nonchalantly to the teacher, "Hey, didja hear the news? Ivadelle slit her own throat with a butcher knife last night."

(Ivadelle Paulson would survive her suicide attempt. She would never return to high school, however. At this writing I have no knowledge of her whereabouts or her life since that tragic moment. Her story still haunts me, and the guilt remains.)

Night Classes For Nobody

History is much too interesting for only public school students to read and study, or so said the new teacher in arguing with the principal. We should have a night class for the students' parents, the teacher argued. Those lucky people could come to the very same classroom their children are in during the day, squeeze into those same chairs, and get the same exciting information at night!

Perversely, the principal balked at adopting this idea. What kind of educator is he? How could any school-man be against adult education?

The pleading to the principal went on for weeks, but no budging. Ahh, he was just too old, too cynical, too out-of-touch to realize how eager older people are to learn! Perseverance finally paid off, however, and the principal caved in to the request, very reluctantly, and with a line about "You'll find out." That first o.k. was all the teacher needed, and he was off and running, first with mimeographed announcements about the night-class sent home with the kids, then a flood of news stories for the local weekly town paper, and even hand-bills were slapped on the telephone poles around town.

The night of the first session of the adult class, the teacher in his new suit and tie was there two hours early arranging and rearranging the chairs, spiffing up the bulletin boards, cleaning blackboards, and dusting maps and globes. The long sign-up sheet was ready, and both questionnaires and history handouts had been printed for one-hundred people, even if the room only held fifty. They would likely have to move to the auditorium to hold the crowd, he believed.

At a quarter to the hour, he awaited the early arrivals seeking a good seat up front where they wouldn't miss anything, but no one arrived early, a bit of a surprise to the teacher. The big surprise came at the exact hour when the class was supposed to start as no one had arrived by that time, either.

Perhaps there was a mistake made in the printed announcements and these were quickly checked. Nope, no errors. The time, date, and place were correct. Everything was correct and ready for the students, except there were no students.

Not one single soul in the community showed up for a night history class. After waiting another long hour, the young teacher reluctantly turned out the lights and walked slowly back to his rooming house, a much wiser person than he had been that morning.

Roger Riistuben

Every day's history class began with current events, all students responsible for two articles that had to be written in sentence form in their news-notebooks. Their news items could include anything newsworthy on the international, national, state or local levels.

Weaning the students as to what was "newsworthy," notably on the local scene, was difficult at first, the students having a perverse desire to relay as "news" all the local dirt and gossip. Sample: "Did you hear that Mrs. Evanson out in the Levis area is having secret meetings with the Omar Breadman?" What went on in the White House was never as "interesting" as what went on in the local country club or taverns. Gradually they improved, however, at least publicly, in their news reporting.

One student, Roger Riistuben, would invariably, for reasons known only to him, report each day on who and how many people got killed in the state's traffic accidents.

Roger became obsessed with having this information so that soon all the other kids would at some point grudgingly ask before the news session ended, "O.K., Big Rog, how many got it on the highways yesterday?" And Roger knew the answer; it was there in his news notebook every day. If the state highway patrol ever lost their records on highway mortalities from September till June, they could go to Roger's notebook for that missing information. Roger Riistuben and the state's traffic fatalities went together. It was odd, peculiar, almost spooky.

(Within a year after his high school graduation, Roger Riistuben was killed in a car crash.)

Supers are Not Super

Superintendents of public schools come and go, and mostly go. In every school district it is the superintendent who is expected to be all things to all people, all groups, everybody! An impossibility. Yet school boards keep looking for that perfect super. He's got to be out there someplace, somewhere, waiting to sign that fat contract — a one year contract, just in case perfection slips from his halo by the end of that first school year. After that, well, "Let him go"; Mr. Right is someone else to be found! Thus did this one neighboring school board keep bringing in for interviews one candidate after another, but alas, all were found wanting in some category and thus fell short of the glory of God, as well as the school district board members. The final candidate interviewed — when the board had reduced the field to ten and decided that all ten weren't worthy enough and decided to start the search all over again from scratch — did make a pithy observation to the board members after being informed that he had fine qualifications but was not really quite the person they were looking for. Said the rejected candidate quietly: "Gentlemen, the only person qualified for you and your position was crucified some two-thousand years ago."

Lester Rierson

(Lines that you're not quite prepared to hear; judgements that are still to be determined.) The principal did not like Lester Rierson. He regarded Lester as a trouble-maker, a hood, a greaser, a thoughtless, selfish and rotten kid who was a good candidate for the state penitentiary.

The new teacher did like Lester Rierson. He regarded Lester as courteous, cooperative, a bright, thoughtful, kind and caring person who was a good candidate for the state university.

One of them was wrong. Which one? That issue was settled this one day in the last period class when the teacher noted Lester's absence and made inquiry to the class members as to Lester's whereabouts. The total silence that followed said more about trouble than any vocal announcement. The kids knew; the teacher did not.

It was during this silence-time when there was a soft knock on the door, and the teacher went to open it. There stood a penitent Lester Rierson in hand-cuffs with two policemen beside him. He then made a bizarre request: "Can I have my assignments for the rest of the year? I've got to go to jail."

(Lester Rierson would be killed the next year in an automobile wreck. It should be noted that immediately after the two-car collision, Lester would be the only victim still conscious, and he personally arranged for as much personal comfort as possible for the other passengers in both cars, after which he walked to a farm house to call the highway patrol. He then walked back to the crash site, checked again the other victims, then sat down along side the road and died from internal injuries.)

The Revenge of the Holsteins

Teacher-training courses in college tell future teachers that "they must be ready for anything" when they get their first teaching job and also that "many things outside of teaching must be done by the teacher." This advice is generalizing, of course, but generalizations are generally true.

Yet even when beginning pedagogues have memorized the above advice to be ready-for-anything, the "anythings" that happen are beyond being ready for.

Case in point. When the new teacher took his winning one-act play cast down to the state capital to participate in the state tournament, it was a cold November day. Nearing the University, their school car managed to get too close behind a large cattle truck, and the car was hemmed in on both sides and behind by other traffic.

This semi-truck was filled with Holsteins, presumably heading for the slaughter-house, but before their demise into roasts and weiners, the critters got a kind of revenge on mankind at that moment by eliminating in large quantities the contents of their kidneys and intestines, which contents flew out through the open truck slats and landed in large quantities all over the school car. It was embarrassing. It was revolting. It was a mess!

It should be noted that windshield wipers do not remove fresh cow dung that splatters and freezes on windshields. It should also be noted that service-station attendants are not interested in removing said dung from school cars. It should further be noted that school-car cleaning is in the category of one of those many strange things outside of the classroom that must be done by the teacher. Yuk. Fie-da. Ish-da.

(Likely the students in that car have long forgotten that incident. Even then the students recovered better and quicker from the cow-trauma than did their teacher. Aside from "that," it was a good trip and a good rating on the play. From that four-person one-act play cast are today a Lutheran minister, a high school counselor, a legal secretary, and a Latin teacher.)

Ernest Skowen

Little Ernest Skowen made a major impression on the local public school the very first day he was enrolled in the first grade. What made him such a "remarkable" kid was that at the tender age of six, Ernest could swear like some career Army sergeant.

When other toddlers sat at their tiny desks, their feet not even touching the ground, they would all at some time, of course, make mistakes in their primer and pre-primer work, errors that might cause the tikes to show their frustration and disgust by uttering cries like "Oh, my," and "Shucks," and perhaps, if advanced in their earthly vocabularies, come with a soft "Heck." Not Earnest. When he made an error, the air turned blue.

Tiny Ernie could string together profanities and vulgarities that would have been the envy of General George Patton, one of the greatest cussers of all time. But Ernie didn't know what he was doing. His lines were said with such innocence, such ease, such simple mouthings of verbal no-nos, all said as easily in his tiny voice as adults say, "Good morning."

Reprimands by the teachers were at first met by Ernie with looks of non-understanding; he didn't know what he was saying was wrong. (After some of Ernie's more colorful lines, the teacher would at first caution him on his language, then she'd have to run into her office before she dared to laugh.)

Ernie Skowen would eventually over the years catch on

One of the great cussers of all time . . .

to social graces so that by the time he reached junior high, he was somewhat judicious enough to choose the time and place for his vocal outlets, although at times he slipped, as he did this one day in his history class. The teacher was aghast! Appalled! Mortified! He was not content to simply chastise him and forget it, the teacher took it upon himself to go and see Ernest's parents. It was quite a meeting.

After the initial "Helloes" and small talk, the teacher led carefully to the main point by suggesting that their son was, on rare occasion, a problem in class, a line met halfway through by the father who interrupted to exclaim:

"Whuzat? Ain't that little %#(## s.o.b. behavin' in that %$##&$#### school? Why that ornery, no-good, lowdown, little bastard! If you're tellin' us that Ernest is causin' trouble, I'll tan his .... until it shines like the .... of the orangutan in the Como Park Zoo." He then turned to his wife and said to her in disbelief: "Didja hear that, Ma?"

She heard, all right, and tossed in her own reactions: "Jeeeeeeessussss H. Ceeeeee-rist! I never thunk that our little Ernest was acting like some .... idjut! I'll grab that jerk by the .... and swing him around, and then hang him up on the clothesline by his .... till that .... turd learns some manners," replied Ma, who then stopped her profanity to ask the teacher for specific acts of malfeasance on the part of their sweet offspring, but by then the teacher had already heard all he wanted and knew on the spot why Ernest was Ernest Blue-mouth.

He considered the aphorism: "As the twig bends, so grows the tree," but altered it to fit the occasion: "As the folks swear, so let teachers beware." The teacher beat a hasty retreat, now believing that little Ernie wasn't too %#(## bad a kid, after all.

(Ernest would become a cross-country trucker. Nuff said.)

Leftover . . .
Legacies

People Talk Farm Talk

"You people sure talk funny around here."

"Huh? Yah, maybe we do, then."

"All you locals make constant reference to things strictly rural," said the city boy visiting his country cousin in our Lutefisk Ghetto. "I find it hard to follow you sometimes, and I certainly cannot identify with many of those terms you use."

His point was accurate. And he wasn't being smart-alecky about it either, but his observation did bring us up short. For perhaps the first time we stopped to consider how our choice of words did make regular reference to things connected with farm life, whether someone "was knee-high to a grasshopper," "stubborn as a mule," or "strong as a horse."

That latter word, horse, in fact was a term that got twisted and turned for many a colorful reference: "wild horses couldn't hold him back;" "hey, horse-face, your old lady wears four-buckles;" "what a clod-hopper he is."

Persons with automobiles not quite running right were hollered at to "got get a horse!" And all car engines were judged in terms of "horse power," all this long before Pintos and Mustangs were on the highways. Persons shown the errors of their ways might still rebel and could then expect to hear: "Well, you can lead a horse to water . . . ."

Even the attempts at word-play jokes brought in the four-legged critter: "One night I slept in the barn, and when I woke up I was a little horse."

Occasionally the jokes changed animals and color: "Every Saturday night in our town is Poultry Night. Yup, every woman on the street gets a free goose. Har, Har."

Then there was the double-whammy story, namely

about the doctor who told old farmer Truls Larson that in his opinion, after examination, that he needed an operation, to which Truls replied: "Ay t'ink Ay need anudder opinion," and the doctor shot back: "You're fat as a p-i-g, you eat like a hog and you got the table manners of a brood-sow at the trough. There, Truls, I told you the truth. Now how'd you like them potatoes?"

"Doc," replied a perplexed and annoyed Truls, "Ay t'ink dey din't get all da lye outa dat las' lutefisk yew ate. Yur as full . . . azs a Ca-riss-mas goose."

At times the vivid reference to farm animals were a bit much. A common expression/put-down for non-athletic high school girls was to say, "Ah, she runs like a cow." (If the girl were statuesque, however, "she's built like a brick out-house.")

Our elderly neighbor regularly described the girth of his cousin's fleshy wife by declaring: "Yah, shee's a big heifer, dat's for shoo-er." (Yet even that same neighbor did have the common sense if not the discretion to avoid phrasing his comments so indelicately when in the presence of his cousin's wife — even as she "ate like a horse": and "bellered like a cow" and "cackled like a hen.")

Mothers regularly described their children's bedrooms as "looking like a pig-sty." (Kids complained that their small bedrooms were "chicken-coops.") Finding items lost was as difficult "as looking for a needle in a haystack," and certainly don't ever take things for granted, that's "counting your chickens before they hatch." Getting money out of certain tight souls was like "trying to squeeze blood out of a turnip," and yet one must try always because you just got to "make hay while the sun shines," and things will happen quickly - "in two jerks of a lamb's tail." But scoffers would add: "I'll believe that the day pigs wear lipstick."

Young farm girls often went to the city "to sow their wild oats," with the men in front of the Hardware Store adding the line: "Yah-da, an' hven dey git back home, dey offen pray for a crop-failure. Hoo hoo." To those listeners who might demur at this coarse reference, well then "Dey can put dat in dere cud and chew it." But if the hearers really liked that first line, they might laugh uproariously, although phrased in the local vernacular, "They'd bray like a jack-ass."

When calmed down, they could cite the old saw, advice on how to be 'lady-like': "Whistling girls and crowing hens always come to bad ends."

Our language, from the most indelicate — read vulgar — to the most abstruse — read weird — carried with it the fundamental realities of the farm life.

It turns out that over the years little has changed in language usage for persons with rural backgrounds — you can't take the country out of the boy — despite the long distances of both time and place from the countryside.

In today's biggest city baseball stadiums one can yet hear some fan holler at the opposing team pitcher that "that guy couldn't hit the broadside of a barn." while the opposing batter is another guy "who couldn't hit a bull on the rear with a grain shovel." If the game became very exciting, it would quickly be labeled a "barn-burner."

We still carry on with the terminology that we know so well, the language of our early environment, the terms that give clearer meaning to communication. The words all burst forth so naturally; they're our inheritance.

Even our own children — whose closeness to an actual farm comes primarily from viewing the same through a window of a car traveling down some interstate highway — those same small boys who have forgotten to zip up their pants are still being told: "Your barn door is open," and maybe even worse: "The horse is getting out."

But now it's time to "put an egg in your shoe, and beat it." Or as the rabbit said when asked if he was ready to go: "Lettuce."

Finding Hidden Water Holes on City Streets

They are usually called "dowsers" but some people call them "water-witchers." Whatever their title, these rare persons have the alleged ability to find water underground by feeling the presence of that water many feet below the ground they're walking on.

To determine exactly where to dig for a well, some dowsers use a forked branch from a willow tree; some use a home-made "fork" made of nylon; others use galvanized wire or coat hangers or a pair of pliers, pendulums, a piece of wood, any Y-shaped instrument to help them "feel" the water. And some dowsers simply determine the closeness of water by the palms of their hands.

To the true believers, dowsing works; it's been used time and time again. To the non-believers, it's a fraud, something passed off as a voodoo gift-of-power when in reality the witchers only make educated guesses and then afterwards claim special gifts after successfully observing a previous set of similar conditions.

The clash between believers and non-believers has led to some curious situations, including one time and place when even non-believers were so desperate that they too were willing to give dowsers a chance. The case involved "lost" city manhole covers.

Among the definitions of a city is this curious sentence: A city is a sewer, by which is meant that whenever a community gets to a point in size where a sewer-system is put in, then the town has reached the growth whereby it takes on the problems connected with any city.

And it was a problem in this one semi-small country town when progress arrived in the form of a new sewer and water system, a project that many of the old timers in town had objected to — "So what's wrong wit' da two-holers in da back yard then?" — while the younger set supported the decision as a major step towards modern times: "This former two-horse town is going to make it on the map yet!" And the not-so-hidden factor in the decision-making was, of course, higher taxes.

The bond issue had passed, nevertheless. The streets had been dug up, and this situation had created a downtown nuisance for an entire summer as people cross-ed the main street on planks and boards set between

My grandma said water-witchers were in cohoots with the devil . . .

mounds of dirt and sawhorses and signs warning of deep ditches and sewer pipes and even more dirt.

But the project at last had been completed, the sewer pipes laid, the mounds of dirt leveled, and then had come the decision of the town council to put down new layers of asphalt, too, on Main Street. After all, why not a new street to go with a new water and sewer system?

This was all fine and good except for one thing. The asphalt-layers laid down their smooth strips of tar all right, but at the same time they covered all the new manhole covers in the street! This new city may have had a major overhaul downtown but when it was done, no one could find the manholes as they'd all been covered over with six inches of asphalt!

Much embarrassment. What to do? It was agreed after heated debate in the council chambers to hire a dowser, old Rasmus Johnson, to find the missing manholes. Rasmus was a bent old figure seen daily amid the retired crew of men sitting outside the hardware store where they gathered daily to prognosticate on all and sundry issues of the times, including always the weather — " 'Tiss tew vet fer da corn crop dis year, den" — to rumored gypsies in the area — "Dey'll steal da cattle, yew betcha, and put a hex on da farmhouse, dat'e fer shoo-er" — to the cause of the latest fire in a warehouse. The men called it another "friction-fire." That's when a hundred-thousand dollar policy rubs against a ten-thousand dollar building. But when it came to the subject of dowsing, the men were in full support of its validity and regarded one of their own, Rasmus Johnson, as the finest of the lost.

The town-council members hadn't been that sure. The arguments brought forward on dowsing said nothing new that hadn't been debated by any two sides before. "What? Are we going to pay good money to some old fool for some hokus-pokus stuff that no sane man believes in?" . . . "Look, dowsing is for real. Some guys like Rasmus have got the gift. I know it don't sound scientific, but for some it works!" . . . "Well my grandma said that water-witchers were in cahoots with the devil" . . . "Ah come off it. That kina stuff should have ended with the Inquisition." . . . "So maybe Rasmus has found wells for dozens of farmers but I'm still not convinced." . . . "Look, some things are beyond understanding. I know a guy who believes in dowsing but doesn't talk about it because he doesn't want people to think he might be kooky or something." **"Think** he's kooky? I know he's **nuts!"** . . . "Hold it. It's a documented fact that Rasmus has found water after regular well-drillers have failed." . . . "Ah, that's baloney. Him finding water is coincidental luck." . . . "But I talked to a guy who first paid a well-driller 300 bucks and he hit granite; then he got Rasmus to come for 25 bucks and found water right away. Real good water, too."

The arguments finally came down to either giving Rasmus a chance or else digging up half the brand new main street, but the agreement was made on the practical basis of no-find, no-pay. That was just hunky-dory with Rasmus who at ten-dollars a manhole was planning to use his extra easy money for a trip to Minneapolis.

Rasmus had said simply that the sensation in his hands when he found water underground was so strong that he wouldn't need any stick, but his "customers" said they liked to see the rod bend down to the earth so Rasmus agreed to carry a Y-forked willow rod to keep them happy.

Thus the next morning offered the curious sight of old Rasmus Johnson walking up and down Main Street, willow stick in hand, followed by the entire town council along with a few of the street department workers. Rasmus would slowly meander back and forth across the street, and then the willow rod would take a sudden bend downward, after which Rasmus simply nodded and the men with the picks and shovels would immediately begin to dig. And sure enough, where the prong pointed there lay the missing manhole cover underneath.

Dowsing may always be beyond logical explanation, but at that point nobody really cared. All they could agree on is that nothing succeeds like success.

When Doors Went 'Thump' at the Grocery Store

"Go to the store," said the mothers, giving errand-orders to their kids to get on their balloon-tired bikes and pedal downtown to pick up something at the grocery store.

As to money to pay for the products —, "Tell 'im to mark it down," said the moms. Charge-accounts at grocery stores were as American as apple pie.

Going-to-the-store never changed, or so it seemed; nor would the store ever change, or so it seemed. But it has changed and worse. The small-town grocery store has gone the way of the DeSoto, Burma Shave signs, and the five-cent Hershey bar, all disintegrating in the name of money and progress.

Certainly the store has changed in our lutefisk ghetto. It once meant Carl Jorgen's general store, and that simple designation meant that all things necessary for mankind's needs could be purchased within the confines of one small building. If Carl didn't have it, you really didn't need it anyway.

Carl's screen-door always bulged from too many kicks. The door swung open on rusted hinges, closed, thanks to a squeaky spring, and made a thumping sound when it banged behind the customer. The door was opened by pushing on the middle wooden bar where a crooked metal sign advertising Wonder Bread reminded customers and made them wonder why anyone ever brought bread.

"Boughten bread" it was labeled derisively. It was tasteless white air that was devoid of nutrition. Wonder Bread was a silly luxury about as useful and about as much used by the locals as the fox-fur coats that were so popular at the time for rich cafe-society matrons who lived far, far away in homes and places seen only in the newsreels.

Uff da. Buy bread? Only if nobody was watching. Otherwise it was putting-on-the-dog, indeed conspicuous consumption! After all, any local housewife who didn't bake her own bread was neglecting her family and duties, and who knows? — just might be thinking of going off from where she belonged — at home!

(The pickle-yard manager, who personally lived in unholy, henpecked home-hell himself, nevertheless took extreme joy in dishing out hypocritical advice to each and every new bridegroom on how to "keep the old lady in the kitchen where they belong: 'shave their head, pull their teeth, and hide their shoes'." The reason the pickleman and his battle-ax wife had no kids to send to the store was known to all; if one looked hard, one could see the ring in the nose.)

But back to Carl's store. Inside the turn-of-the-century building, there lay a bumpy, sometimes humped, wooden floor whose loose slats heaved and creaked and groaned when walked upon. But it was the smells that hit the customer after that screen door thumped. Wafting aromas filled the nostrils, the smells of mouth-watering chubby hams hanging silently on ropes from the ceiling back in one corner; the pungent odors from the spices lying open in counter-bins; the enticing aroma of freshly ground coffee coming from that large red machine with the big silver wheel on the side.

Then there were the open cookie-bins where the power of freshly baked molasses cookies overwhelmed those dainty white sugar cookies that were so delicious when dunked into a cup of coffee. But cookie smells competed only faintly with the powerful scent of home-made baloney and summer sausage, of too-ripe bananas at three cents a pound, of Summertime tobacco in the opened three-pound can, available free to those customers who wanted one pinch to chew and two pinches to smoke in a corncob pipe.

For the kids on errands the very best smells mingled in the distinctive odor of the candy-counter where sticky red and white peppermint canes hung on white string from flour sacks, where hard black licorice came at a penny a foot, where there were penny candies of all shapes and sizes — five cents' worth would fill up a small bag, and a whole quarter's purchase produced quantities for the whole week's eating orgy.

In the middle of the dimly-lit store stood a small island, a horseshoe shaped counter dominated by a large cast-iron register that opened with a growl and a clang and a ding when anyone turned the big crank on the side.

And there behind the counter stood the owner, Carl, fat Carl, his curly hair parted in the middle, Carl peering intently over the top of his black, dime-store-bought glasses and trying to decipher the latest note from some mother, a note written in hieroglyphics on half a sheet of coarse paper ripped out of a tablet, a grocery-order which was to send the kid home immediately with a bagful of groceries.

While Carl lumbered about his establishment — the kid's order-slip in one hand, the order itself juggled and balanced in the other arm — the kid ogled and squirmed and anguished in front of the candies trying to make the tough decision of going for the penny-stuff or blowing the whole buffalo-head on a box of Crackerjacks in hopes of getting a stupendous prize inside the box. Las Vegas gamblers never took bigger risks than a kid going for Crackerjacks.

The order filled, Carl took from a shoe box the family charge-account pad and marked each item boldly with a carpenter's pencil, with the yellow carbon-slip then placed on top of the order. The transaction completed, the screen door thumped behind another satisfied customer.

Carl himself was a distinctive figure. He looked like a small-town merchant was supposed to look, complete with long white apron, wide suspenders holding up his too-large pants, a white shirt with a leather, black bow tie, and black armbands holding back the drooping sleeves from getting into the peanut butter as he spooned it out in pound lots from the tin container. (And there was always a little fresh blood on his apron, as Carl was a butcher in every sense.)

Despite the use of the most modern automobiles, Carl drove only his Model-T Ford touring car, even if the top was gone, and this clackety machine he used both summer and winter. And always in the passenger side beside Carl was his constant companion, Ole, a Dachshund weiner-dog to which Carl spoke only in Norwegian.

Indeed, all the dog understood was Norsk and the locals knew this so that when they wanted to call Ole they didn't say "Come here, doggie;" it was "Com hit, du, hund." Ole was Carl's shadow. (And sadly it might be noted that both dog and master were to pass away within a short time of each other.) The dog, the store, the Model T, Carl — they were all a part of each other. They're all gone now.

Historians are not much for predictions. The only safe thing they can forecast is that things will change; that's the only sure sign in their crystal ball, change.

Certainly "the store" changed. Now instead of ownership being indicated by a hand-made, paint-peeling sign above the screen door, there's out front by the street a garish electric sign that lights up automatically when dusk slides into the Scandinavian night.

Instead of hearing the creak of springs and the thump of a door closing, there is today the low hum of a glass door sliding open before the customer touches it.

Today there are no groaning wooden floors; there are instead cream-colored tiles that shine antiseptically like some hospital corridor, and at the entrance is something that looks like fake green grass to wipe your shoes on.

Conspicuous by absence are the smells of foods. Almost all items are wrapped in plastic, notably the meats which lie in low-humming freezers with no doors. Any food smell that might escape into the store air is eliminated by air fresheners. Not even the whiff of peppermint candy is allowed to escape as that too is enclosed in plastic.

Today people buy that Wonder Bread, and it's a wonder if anyone bakes the homemade kind anymore.

Cash registers don't growl and rumble and there's no cranking required to get the cash-drawer open with a clang and ding. Today if there's any sound at all it's a click-click-click while little square numbers flash up on a tiny screen while an impassive, unknown clerk tallies the items. And if the customer might say to "mark it down," the next likely words would be "I'll call the Manager!" Charging groceries today is un-American.

Most people say that the new store is "good for business" and that the town "is making progress" and "isn't that air-conditioning wonderful?" Perhaps. Still, Carl — and Ole — it's probably a good thing you're gone. You wouldn't like the progress. And the boughten bread is still awful.

The High School Star at His Very Best

"Why do many people deliberately choose to live in small rural towns?" ask curious or doubtful or disdainful city dwellers. This is a reasonable question that can perhaps be answered in part by citing small town events — like a recent high school graduation in our lutefisk ghetto.

The school gymnasium had taken on a different look to meet the requirements of a different situation. Because it was graduation for thirty-seven students, the regular gym was supposed to look like, well, an auditorium, and if you don't have the latter, well you sort of dress up what's available.

On the edge of the gym stage stood vase after vase of fresh lilacs which offered a delightful aroma even if the common purple flowers may not have resembled orchids. Even better than the flowers on the stage was a small table piled high with diplomas which were not arranged alphabetically. There was no need for that. The principal knew everybody: so did the school board: indeed, everybody knew everybody.

Also on the stage was a small group of ten men appearing to look ill at ease and out of place and certainly out of uniform, the school board members. The open shirts and often overalls worn at the regular board meetings had given way to tightly buttoned white shirts and wide ties and blue suits and brown shoes.

The graduates, of course, in their black gowns with the mortarboards sitting at all angles on carefully coiffed heads, sat impatiently on gray metal folding chairs in the front rows waiting and waiting for the years' old ritual to move along quickly so they could hustle out of that stuffy gym with their diplomas in hand and move on to their graduation parties.

To all appearances it was a common, routine scene matched a thousand times over in similar gyms in similar towns. But this was different. Amid the small sea of black gowns sat Danny Bekadahl. By usual measurements Danny should not have been there. Danny had more problems going for him than should befall any young lad: mental retardation, physical retardation, vocal retardation, and a contorted body easily given to seizures, especially when he got nervous.

Graduations, of course, can be nervous times for everyone. Danny would not receive the usual diploma but instead get a special certificate that had been prepared for him - if he could make it through the ceremonies.

Danny, as part of graduation, was a calculated risk that the seniors themselves had asked to take. After all, Danny was one of them, had been for twelve years: they had collectively helped to raise him or at least pulled him along with them throughout their schooling. But what might happen? What might he do to disrupt and maybe ruin the ceremonies?

And who would sit beside the squirming Danny? That turned out to be the least of the problems as the class star athlete - a National Honorary Society member - and the class valedictorian volunteered to have Danny placed between them.

Things went well with Danny and everybody from the initial procession of the straining band-sounds of Pomp and Circumstance" through the primarily female chorus singing the wrenching "Halls of Ivy." When it appeared that the pent-up Danny might erupt, the soft voice of the handsome athlete and his gentle hand on Danny's knee kept him calm enough to remain in control.

Then came the moment everyone dreaded for Danny. One by one the seniors were called by name and one by one they left their chairs, marched up the steps to the stage to receive their diplomas from the school board chairman.

Near the end of this portion of the ceremony Danny's name was called. Now he had to be alone. He struggled to move out of his seat and managed further to struggle up those five steps alone. Then he stood by himself in the center of the stage and turned around, a frightened look on his face.

The large audience until that moment had been busy buzzing and fanning themselves with programs. Now everyone and everything was quiet, absolutely silent. The whole gym came to a halt. What would happen?

In the long seconds following, the stillness and panic was broken by the reassuring quiet voice of the athlete who stood on the edge of the stage and had looked back: "It's all right, Danny. Go ahead. We're still with you."

That was all it took. Danny limped over to the chairman, received his certificate, got a big handshake and stepped back with the biggest smile on his face that anyone could imagine. At that very moment the entire audience stood as one for a thunderous ovation of applause.

It was all over. Danny moved easily back to his chair but it took a while to get there because classmate after classmate had to stop; and hug him and give him kisses and pump his hand. Finally he was back to his chair, back to another reassuring pat on the leg from the athlete beside him along with a whisper in the ear which made Danny smile broadly again.

In another twenty-five years the only thing likely to be remembered about the class of '85 graduation will be the warmth and humanity of a community in general and the genuine kindness and compassion of the class star athlete in particular. This quiet, self-effacing young man had quarterbacked his team to the team conference championship, had set a school scoring record in bringing his school to the state basketball tournament, and at graduation time he was in the middle of pitching his squad towards a state baseball tournament. And yet this gentle giant had never starred more on a playing field or a basketball floor than he did at his own graduation. His was a great performance, one that shall long be remembered.

addendum: The name of the athlete is John Moe. He would attend the community college at Glendive, Montana, that fall where he had received a full-ride basketball scholarship.

For photograph of John Moe, see page 197

The (Im)Purity of Language

Americans traveling to the Scandinavian countries to visit their ancestral homes — and looking up shirt-tail relatives — practically an article of faith to be carried out by many Upper Midwest citizens.

Every summer Americans by the thousands descend on the old-world sod, and once there, some of them try out the native tongue, with mixed results, of course. Language can be a problem for all American travelers in Europe.

All of the above is commonplace. What is becoming more common is for Scandinavians to come to America to visit their relatives and try out their English on their Midwestern cousins. That can be a problem on this end, too, even when visitors think they know English very well.

Such was the case for twenty-five year old Halvard Grona who decided to travel from his home city of Bergen in Norway and accept a longstanding invitation from his American aunt and uncle to visit them.

In planning for his visit, Halvard had been motivated to learn good English because he had personally heard over and over again Americans in Norway struggling to communicate in Norwegian, and usually failing. At some point the Americans would become exasperated and resort to English while at the same time hunting for someone to translated for them. Uff da. That was about the only line both sides understood.

Halvard Grona didn't want to be that kind of foreign visitor in the United States. He planned and prepared carefully to speak perfect English, a plan which included his spending a year at Oxford University in England, and there he learned English — the Queen's English — which he believed would serve him perfectly when he arrived by

They talked better Norsk than Halvard heard at home . . .

plane in Minneapolis for a month's visit with relatives. He was wrong.

Within two minutes on U.S. soil, Halvard knew that all his preparation for oral communication was a failure. His aunt and uncle didn't speak English, they talked 'Merican at best and Midwest-Mare-kin at worst. In this curious situation, each side thought the other talked goofy, and there was some doubt as to which one was the foreigner. Uff da.

"Halvar'! 'S'good ta-see ya got 'roun ta gettun to our rejun. Nize ta ha visders from Scin-ayv-yah. Not minny fern-ners come to our li'l siddy," said Uncle Harold, giving him a big greeting at the airport.

"Yah, we wuz list'nen to the ray-joe drivun," added Aunt Florence, "an dere's a sterm a'comun frum south'here, near Duh-Moyne. Dat's da cabbadull of I'way."

Uncle Harold chimed in again to add more verbal confusion. "Dat plane wuz layder den we planned fer. 'Sides da wedder iss tuff. 'S'wors'nigh thought. An' we hadda dodge murrn'cy vickul, an am blunts headun hell-bent for sum hos-pal. Musta bin a lady havun a kid on'a'way."

After picking up Halvard's suitcases, the three of them got in Harold's car — "a Ferd" — and began driving away from the big siddy towards a smaller city and then their farm. Florence spoke quickly to her husband and when he didn't respond immediately, she said it again. "Aright, I hurja da furs time," and all she had said was that he had to stop at the grocery store so she could "picka pounda budder up."

Harold's car swung quickly around a Cadillac and he commented to Halvard that he wished he could afford such "a lug jury."

"How's she goin' in Yerp?" asked Harold of the new confused arrival beside him.

"Europe?" said Halvard, wondering if he had the right translation. "Europe is a continent full of chahm," he replied. "A bit pooky, though."

Now Harold was wondering if he had the right translation. "Well, dunno 'bout all dat, but fern-fairs comeszup in diz-cussions now'nden, expechully Leb-non or Mare-ka's allies whin dey're fightun dem Rooskies."

Halvard at that moment looked at the car's gas gauge. "Ah say, Uncle, it appears that you are a bit low on petrol. Bloody low, Ah'd say."

"Yah shoo-er, yew betcha. But ain'zacklee out yet. Got plen'y gas, and more in da 'chine-shed a' home. Daz one of da out'bild-ins on 'a farm."

"Wire you doin that?" said an annoyed Aunt Florence. "Par'n me, cuz 'member lass cheer when ya ran-otta-gaz? I say stop in town an' I'll git budder while you git gaz an' then le's go to a resternt an' have sumpun ta eat."

"Lis'n, woman. I buys hunnerts o' gallons, maybe t'ousins, and I know dis jalopy! We'll make'er awright, yew betcher boots."

Halvard was sorry he even mentioned the topic. He thought to divert the gas argument — at least he thought the issue was over petrol — by bringing up the topic of American politics. "Pity the way Americans fight over politics. Pity. By the way, Uncle, was not this a Presidential election year in this country?"

"You bet! Dere wuss so minny presdenshul can-dates an' plit'cull vizders runn' roun' yu'd think every guy an' his brudder wanza move to Wash'n'tin. An' we got gummint deaf-sits so az to make yer eyes pop! An' makes no dif-rinse if it's Dimcrats or Raypublicans; bod-a-dem are chuck-full of be-low-nee."

Even if Halvard couldn't understand his Uncle, just the tone of the voice suggested even another subject might be more desirable, so Halvard decided to bring up the one topic that he knew Americans were crazy about, sports. And sports news.

"Sport snooze?" said Florence. She had news all right. "We gotta grrrreat girls' baskiball team! Bin playun toged-der since kinnergarden. Got dis one bean-pole kid who wearza nicklis, earrins and Jewry, ekcetera. Makes ya won'er 's'worl's'comun'to."

All this foreign English was more than Halvard could handle. It was harder for him to decipher than Swahili.

Even ten Webster dictionaries wouldn't help; and the same number of atlases wouldn't allow him to find states like Nordakoda, or cities like Dooloot or Mad'sin or Minnaplis, even if he took the suggestion of his uncle to "lis'n real careful-like and brush up on some disnull vocablarry frum books in da liberry."

So ten more miles down the road, Halvard decided to do what Americans did in Bergen, resort to the language they knew best, but in his case it was Norwegian. He didn't want to do it, but after all the communication gap had to be broken. What then followed was remarkable in every way. Not only did his aunt and uncle speak good Norwegian, they spoke PURE Norwegian! They talked better Norsk than Halvard heard at home!

In Norway, because of the many shifting regional dialects that had infiltrated everyday language, along with the ongoing fight there between the official Ny Norsk (new Norwegian) and Landsmal (old Norwegian), the purity was gone. It had gone to Amerika!

Halvard Grona found it curious and ironic and wonderful that he had to go to a foreign country to hear Norwegian spoken so well. After this discovery they had great conversations and a fine time; the communication gap was broken.

In his month's stay, Halvard and his uncle and aunt would eventually have many good laughs over the subject of language, with Harold reminding him: "If you t'ink we talk funny-like, den, ya-da go down to Al'bamy. Den turn 'roun' and head Nort' an' East an' lis'en ta dem nuts i' New Yersey."

"Uncle," responded Halvard, "Someday I'm coming back and learn the toughest variation of English spoken, and then I can participate in your favorite conversational topics: 'da timpitcher, da schurch, 'lectric rates, an' all da sports snoose.' "

"Uff da."

The Pattern of Change in 'Eating Out'

Recently we had visitors for a week from Norway, a couple from Lena, in the Toten district just north of Oslo. In their month's stay in America, not too much surprised this husband and wife, with one exception: the degree to which Americans go outside their homes to eat.

Our Norwegian visitors were pleasantly shocked at the extent to which American restaurants are patronized at all hours of the day or night. They at first found it almost impossible to believe that people in the USA went out even for breakfast!

Implicit in this surprise, of course, is the fact that Norwegians, at least as whole families, seldom go out to dine in restaurants. Eating, socializing, moderate social drinking are things to be done in the homes. Hence "a big meal out" invariably means going to somebody's house for a special meal.

The reasons for Norwegians not going to some cafe are both economic and cultural. To order a single T-bone steak dinner, for example, in Bergen — a meal that might include wine and dessert — would cost one at least fifty dollars. It's very expensive to eat out in Norway, as many a tourist can attest.

But the culture of Norway also decrees that homes are the settings for proper socializing and good dining. It is also proper that housewives be prepared to make special meals super-special. Home-cooking remains a Norwegian art form, even if the results are often whitish in color, whether it's romegrot or flour-gravy.

Naturally this ethnic trait has carried over to the new world. The whole idea of "going out to eat" — or rather

NOT going — was very strong in our lutefisk ghetto, too, in the years around World War II. "Going out to eat" then meant stopping at a cafe for a cup of coffee and a fry-cake (do-nut) or a piece of pie. The only people who actually ate full meals in restaurants were traveling salesmen or local bachelors and widowers who were either too lazy or incompetent to cook for themselves.

But for a father to take his family out, say, on Friday night after work for a full meal of meat and potatoes? Never! Families ate at home! They might have snacks at a restaurant but no more. Amen and uff da.

In discussing family eating habits with others who grew up in the 1940's, it seems apparent that the stay-home-and eat attitude was widespread. A man from Gary, South Dakota — now a top man with Otter Tail Power Company — said the first time he ever went to a restaurant for a meal happened when his high school musical group went to a neighboring town for a band tournament. He and his friends were given a stipend and told to get some dinner. When they got inside the eatery, he was handed something he had never seen before, a menu. The young diner from Gary was so confused and flustered by all this that when the waitress came to take his order, he announced "I'll have what everybody else is having." A hot-beef sandwich and a glass of milk was the result: it cost thirty-five cents.

I had never eaten a full restaurant meal with my parents until the year I started college in 1949. On our way to Luther College in Decorah, Iowa, we stopped in LaCrosse at The Bodega (when it's your first time, you remember the name and all the details). It was cafeteria-style and the father told his nervous and confused but famished son (me) to help himself to as much as he wanted, a statement he regretted as I loaded my tray to the collapsing point, trying to make up in one sitting for all the years previously missed. I mean taking banana, apple, and blueberry pies for dessert stretched both the pocketbook and the waistline.

Those Depression Years, of course, had scarred all

Americans. There was scarcely enough money for basic food at home, let along going out to some cafe. I didn't know we were poor in the Depression until I got older and had left home. I suppose I should have been depressed by this poverty but concluded that most families we knew were in the same boat and had managed to survive all right. Turned out that we had everything we needed in our family except money.

Even in those good economic years after the war the old habits changed little. Kids then did not know what going out to eat was like, but we didn't miss it because we had never done it in the first place. Conversely, our own children have known little but restaurant-eating as part of growing up. Our one hungry kid learned how to say Shrimp before she could say Mother. And none were the least bit impressed by the old man's tale of his FIRST MEAL AT THE BODEGA at age eighteen: they just acted bored and mumbled ya-ya-ya and reached for the menu while they decided whether it should be steak and lobster — or both!

Now in retrospect, and considering the many bucks that have poured out of a thinning wallet in some fancy dining place, maybe the Norwegians are right after all. But watch out, Norway; Oslo now has its first MacDonald's! Can Wendy's, Hardee's, Burger King, Perkin's and Taco John's be far behind? I hope so.

Home-Made Medicines
Now Dey'd Cure Anything, Den

Three old men sat hunched and huddled together in the corner of the waiting room. Seated in nondescript worn and faded plastic chairs, they deliberately slouched forward to better hear each other. And the better to complain to fellow sympathizers.

Their complaints centered on current medical practices in general and their own aches and pains in particular. They didn't much go for either category. Their aging bodies — all were in their seventies — were wearing out, their bones arthritic, their joints stiff. But their tongues worked just fine.

"All these new fangled medicines we take these days is so much wasted money," declared Ivar Rosaack as he hoisted his gimpy leg into a more comfortable position.

"They say to exercise more," he continued, "but I had enough hard work in my day to last me two lifetimes. Men these days don't know what hard work is! They're soft. And when I see grownup men running around the block — jogging I think they call that foolishness — well I just gotta shake my head an' wonder if those nuts have got all their marbles."

"Das fer shoo-er," nodded Ingemund Peterson, who added: "An' dey lewk naked asz a yay-bird. And mos' uf dem iss so skinny dat Ay'd like to take'em home and giff'em a square meal, den."

"Yah, you betcha," added the third man, Gudbrand Gudmansen, "an' they wear those goofy-looking shoes that are blue or red or green and even yellow! Jeepers-creepers, in our day when we saw a man wearing tennis shoes on the streets, the guy was either a wino or a welfare case."

"And most of them famous joggers on TV look so sickly! Remind me of starving dogs. It's s'posed to make them healthy, but looks to me like they could all use some vitamins and some pep-up medicine, like maybe molasses. That's what our Ma gave us kids for energy, black molasses." " 'Member those home medicines we used to take? People can laugh, but they was better than those pink pills these young whipper-snapper doctors prescribe for us now," declared Gudbrand.

"You bet!" replied Ivan with gusto. "My Maw she used garlic for when we got sick. House stunk so bad sometimes the neighbors wouldn't come in. And we smelled so stout in school that the teacher made us sit in the hall-entry. Cured us, though."

"If you think you stunk from garlic, you should have smelled our hired man." said Gudbrand. "He was bald-headed. Bald as a melon. Anyhow, someone once told him there was only one thing that would work to restore hair — and the fool used it. He gobbed on skunk-oil! Holy-ol'-golden! You could smell him downwind a mile away. Ma made him sleep in the hay mow."

"Well," said Ivan not appreciating the interruption, "My Maw she sometimes used camphor oil for colds. And if the cold hung on, we got to drink a mixture of hot wine and cinnamon sticks — or brandy and hot water mixed with sugar and lemon."

"Vell, den, in our house — 'causs my Granpa wuss a Finnlander — we wuss all sent to da sauna if ve got a cold. Heck, den, ve vent to da sauna for effryt'ing! "Sauna-sulphur-and-pitch' wuss Gramp's motto to cure anyt'ing. Uff da, but he wuss a tuff guy, tew. If he cut himself, he put horse urine on it. And if a deep cut needed stitches, he sewed himself up wit' string from a flour sack," concluded Ingemund, with head shaking.

By now the three men were on a roll and forgetting about their own medicines; they were more interested in the old ways of the old days and their fondly-remembered home-remedies that combined ersatz medicine, superstition and religion.

"It was roots and herbs all boiled together into a thick broth. That's what we got for bad stomachs," recalled Ivan. "And when we got styes on our eyes, Maw put tea bags over 'em. And for a bad headache she wrapped a wool-sock poultice around our head that was filled with sliced raw potatoes and onions all soaked in vinegar."

"Well, we had to wear a scratchy wool sock around our neck everytime we got a sore throat," said Gudbrand, "and a bread-and-milk poultice worked fine too for drawing out boils - and I dasn't forget the mustard plaster."

"Vell, Ay t'ink a side-pork poultice vorked better den bo'd of yur cures," said Ingemund, trying to outdo the others.

Ivan was not listening. He was thinking about his childhood. "Now those were hard days, we all remember that. After the war when your family got a few bucks, then Maw bought Vicks-Vapo-Rub. She rubbed that grease on so thick and so hard that I thought the Vicks goop was gonna come through me on the other side. Worked though."

"Well, when we got a little money," said Gudbrand, not to be left out of the changing time-periods, "Pa bought olive oil and heated it and poured it into our ears for earaches. And for general hearing purposes generally, worked, too. Yes it did. 'Course for nervous stomachs Pa and Ma both went with the old way for a cure. It was orange-peels ground up and mixed with coffee-grounds. I 'member gettin' a nervous stomach just waitin' to get that stuff that was s'posed to cure my nervous stomach."

"When it came to stomach troubles we used parsley in all forms," said Ivan. "And I recall my baby brother getting diaper rash, and Maw put tallow and chicken grease on his little bottom. Fixed 'im right up too, you darn tootin' it did."

"You remember the Watkins Man coming around? That travelin' salesman had cures for any thing." recalled Gudbrand. "My Ma's favorite was Lydia Pinkham, and also Carter's Little Liver Pills, and at that time — I was justa wee tike — I wondered if those pills were for big livers too.

Ha ha, I wuz kinda dumb then."

"Vell den, yew gice kin talk medicine curess, but my uncle Thorleff he sess dat it wus **evil-spir'ts** dat made persons sick. Da sick had hexes,and da only vay ta cure 'em wuss to un-hex 'em. Uncle Thorleff sess: 'Let da evil return to da outside uf da body!' Dass hvat he sess," said Ingemund, who sat back after that line,j figuring he outdid both of them with that hex stuff.

"I'm glad you brought that up about evil-spirits, 'cause once we lived next farm over from a immigrant German-Russian family. Hoot-te-too! Now was they ever hooked on the mumbo-jumbo business of good health," said Ivan, who was off and running about his neighbors.

"The whole family mumbled all kinds of little sayings and rhymes to ward off cuts and bruises. And the old folks always talked about 'having to have the faith' in order to get healed. No faith, no cure. Sure if I didn't once see the mother breath into the mouth of her sick child and call on the Trinity three times to cure him!"

"Ah, you're foolin' us now," said a scoffing Gudbrand.

"No sir-ee-sir, I ain't. Honest-Injun! It even got worse than that, 'cause I know when somebody got real real sick in that German-Russian house, they called in from another district a kind of medicine-man-like kind of special healer called a 'Brauge," and then the real hocus-pocus-belly-okus stuff started.

"Ay t'ink yew pullin' our legs, den, Ivan. 'Tiss pagan-stuff dat iss."

"Now hold on! It's true. I swear it. And before you get so darn holy, read Luke 8: 42-43 and you'll find that Jesus was the first blood stopper. But with this same family it did get a little creepy. Like they believed that the touch of a dead man's hand would cure anything from ringworm to gout."

"In that case," said Gudbrand "I think, Ivan, that you should take that limpy leg of yours down to the under-taker and maybe Digger Dahlen can find a dead hand or two to lay on you. Har har," laughed Gudbrand.

"No thank-you; that's going too far, but I tell you I'll still take our old home remedies anytime over today's purple pills in those tiny bottles with words on 'em so long you can't pronounce 'em, let alone know what they mean."

"Dass fer shoo-er," agreed Ingemund. "Gimme da ol' stuff inytime, den."

"Me too. I'm with both of you," concluded Gudbrand. "Modern medicine ain't no good."

Just then the door to the waiting room opened and out stepped a young lady in a white uniform. "Which one of you is Mr. Peterson?" asked the pretty nurse.

"Dass me, Miss."

"Fine. The doctor will see you now. Also the doctor said to tell you other two that you can both get your prescriptions refilled when the pharmacy opens in two minutes."

"Well, then," said Ivan a little sheepishly, "at least the Doc ain't no 'Brauge.' C'mon let's git our pills and then head down to the Taproom and git into a whist game. All this medicine-talk makes me feel worse than ever."

Scandinavian Maids in Evanston;
(Turkeys Are for Rare Stuffing)

There is a major theme in Norwegian-Americanism that has been barely scratched by historians, and that theme involves the large numbers of Norwegian-American young, single girls who left their rural farm homes to go to the cities, especially to Evanston, Illinois, to take jobs as domestic servants in private homes.

There were young ladies of other ethnic backgrounds, of course, who also went to work as maids in "the big city," but Scandinavians were notably high proportionately and in the total numbers of home-helpers in Evanston during the decades of the 1920s and 1930s and before.

In the region surrounding our lutefisk ghetto, it was commonplace for families to either have someone themselves or certainly know someone who had gone off to work in the city as a maid. This kind of work was socially acceptable for young women in a time period when employment opportunities for females was considerably limited.

Getting a maid's job was often an economic necessity. In the Depression Thirties, it was no great secret that many farm families depended on their daughters in the cities to save the farmstead by sending enough money home to pay the real estate taxes, and maybe add a little on the mortgage, too.

Prior to the departure of any youth, it was a common joke of the Depression for the remaining family members to say, "Write when you get work." There was a lot of economic truth in that line for the folks back home.

In order to achieve a solid history of these rural girls off to the city, there is a need for research, interviews, especially oral histories of dozens of these women who are nowadays up in years and mostly retired, if they're alive at all. More oral histories would add a significant contribution to the ongoing larger study of Scandinavians in America. Such a project would make a valuable contribution.

The remainder of this article deals with an interview with one such lady who left her farm home in central Wisconsin at age 17 ("I lied my age") and went off to be a maid in Evanston.

The person interviewed was age 71 at the time — and she thought we were just "visiting" about "the old days" — and a family relative, but not likely would she want her name mentioned, despite the wonderful tale she told.

Importantly, she viewed her own experiences as entirely typical of what her other maid friends went through, and thus her comments are likely representative of a large sampling.

Our "visiting" was largely one of many questions for her to answer:

Did you leave the farm and go to the city without having any leads on a job?

"Oh, no. We got copies of the **Evanston Review** and studied those help-wanted sections back home on the farm, and then we wrote letters off. Pa wouldn't just let us go unless we had something to go to."

When you arrived in the city, was there someone to meet you at the station?

"Yah, it seemed like half our township at home had somebody already there, so that helped and made you feel safer to see a familiar face when you got off the train."

Once you arrived in Evanston, then what?

"Then we'd hit the streets walking and more walking and go to those big houses along those streets with all the big elm trees and go up to those fancy doors and knock. And hope."

When did you first go there?

"Let's see, I was just 17 the first time I went. I lied about my age. You were s'posed to be 18. That was 1932, Most girls went there for what they called 'the season', that is the months of the school year. That's what I did. Some went only to work in the summer time but that's when I went back home to the farm. I always told 'em my folks needed me, which they kinda did."

What family gave you your first job in 1932?

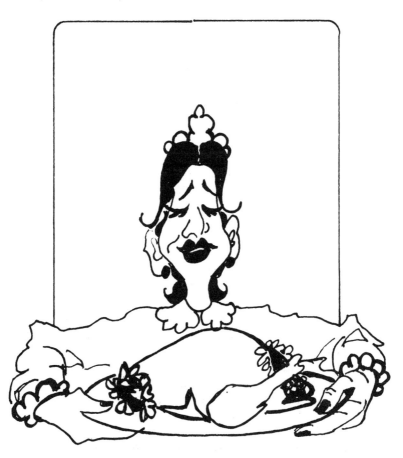

I thought slavery . . . ended in this country . . .

"It was a doctor and his wife. He was some kind of special surgeon. They had two little kids. Real brats."

What was your salary?

"FIVE DOLLARS A WEEK! And for that measly amount they had me doing everything! Clean and sweep and cook and clean some more, and this was seven days a week!"

Did you get any time off from work?

"Yup, on Thursday and Sunday afternoons. That was it. And by the time I got the noon dishes done and the kitchen cleaned up, it was three o'clock before I could get out of there! And then when I'd get back to the house they'd have left me another pile of dishes to do. Oh, **Herre Gud!** (Holy God)."

Did you wear a uniform?

"You bet. A little gray one most of the time, but for a real fancy dinner party with guests, it was a black one."

Were those maid's dresses provided for you?

"No way! We had to buy our own. On a lousy five bucks a week!"

Was it hard work for the maids?

"Depended on the people. Now that first family I was with, she was a real witch! She had me doing something every minute of the day and night."

How were you treated otherwise? Were you made to feel comfortable and part of the household?

"Nope. In fact, I thought at the time that slavery was supposed to have ended in this country."

How so?

"Well, here's a case. For the big meal they always had meat — which I'd prepared, of course - but the husband wanted to cut it up, to carve it himself in front of everybody. So I'd stand there by the dining room table and watch him saw away, making pieces for everyone's plate and then passing them the plate. Then I'd be handed my little piece and then turn around and head back into the kitchen. You were made to feel like you were nothin'."

How did you know when you were to return to the dining room during meals?

"There was a little bell that rung in the kitchen. Some kind of gadget under the table in the dining room got pushed with your foot, and when the bell rung, I had to stop whatever I was doing and hurry in there."

As a maid, did those kids give you special problems?

"Sure did, until they learned who was boss when their parents left the house. About the first night I got there they left, and this little boy refused to go to bed when told, so I let him have it with a hairbrush."

Did the little boy report you later

"Guess not. I kept my job."

Did the other young maids who were your friends have similar situations where they worked?

"Yah, purdy much. As I said, the work was much the same but of course the people you worked for were always different. Like this first doctor's family. Gawd! That woman was as witch! But the others later were better. I shoulda done to this doctor-family what my one friend did to hers. Hoo-hoo, that would have showed 'em."

What happened?

"Well, they treated her like dirt all year long, and it was Thanksgiving coming up, and her birthday too, and for a birthday present they gave her a maid's uniform! For a birthday present! Just the thing she hated. Well, that did it! Anyway, she did prepare this great big Thanksgiving dinner and worked like a dog to get it ready, but inside the turkey, instead of putting in stuffing, she stuck that maid's uniform, and then she walked out the back door and never came back!"

. . . .

Final thought. One of the great, if improbable, reunions in the near future could be that of all the Scandinavian women in America who once worked as domestic servants in Evanston in the 1930s. Northwestern University there could play host, open up their large gymnasium — (would it require the football stadium?) — and simply permit the ladies to swap stories and exchange experiences as they'd reminisce about "the bad old days," which likely wouldn't seem so bad anymore. At the same time they're telling stories, they would be relating some exciting history, too, and have one whee of a good time. In this possible situation of storytelling, one wonders if any lady at that reunion could top the incident of the maid's dress stuffed in a turkey carcass? It would be fun to find out.

Destruction
At the Altar Railing

Certain social and religious ceremonies expect certain behaviors. Some rituals occurring within an institutional framework require appropriate solemnity on everyone's part. Such are the conditions, for example, involving participants receiving communion at church services.

The Lord's Supper, The Eucharist, Holy Communion — whatever the title — is a major sacrament in every Christian denomination. The time for the distribution of the bread and wine to bowed, kneeling communicants is indeed a serious moment. At least it should be.

It is understood by almost everyone that communion is not the time for extraneous comments, let alone levity and backtalk. Kneeling at the altar rail is neither the time nor the place to question pastoral functions, utter tangential asides, nor ask dumb questions in a loud voice, all of which alone or collectively can destroy the entire formality of the occasion.

But it can happen, and did. By a little old lady. Not purposely, not with malice aforethought on the part of the destroyer, no planned challenge to the ages-old liturgy coming from an elderly verbal-vandal whose timing was devastating.

It happened in a nursing home chapel service when Olga Johanneson, age 85, royally ruined a Sunday morning for the entire congregation. It was quite a performance.

Her performance should not be declared successful as this suggests a positive outcome. Olga's contribution was negative and the outcome was a disaster. It would become the talk of the town for years afterwards.

Were it not for the young Lutheran minister adapting quickly to Olga's whims and outbursts that day, enough at least to get her to finally shut up and sit down, it might have gone down in history as a tragedy. But it wasn't. In fact, it was kind of fun.

The pastor's ability to laugh at it after — but not during — the church service ended makes the event thus eligible for a special award in some Guinness book of records.

* * * *

Olga Johnson was not really a mean lady bent on creedal destruction, and certainly she was not a deliberate trouble maker, although she was kind of ornery.

At age 85, with hardening of the arteries, Olga was frequently — as her relatives discreetly phrased it — "confused" at times, though which times they were not sure of. Some days, or some minutes of some days, she was not sure of who, where, or what she was, but none of that ever stopped her from talking.

Besides this confusion, Olga could not hear well, and she was too tight, said her elderly son, to buy new batteries regularly for her hearing aid, and so nurses and doctors and fellow residents had to shout to be understood by her. Then again she heard exactly what she wanted to hear. No more, no less.

Her old-fashioned hearing aid device was one in which the receiver hung by a cord around her neck, and being a bit vain about this whole contraption, she hid the receiver inside the toe of a long, cotton stocking, which also got wrapped around her neck, the toe lying on her bosom. Those who really wanted to be understood totally had to get their faces down so that their noses practically touched her bust.

Her combination of problems kept Olga from going regularly to church services. She was both stubborn and independent and normally said and did exactly as she pleased, including church attendance decisions.

This one Sunday was Communion-Day and Olga was determined to attend for reasons known only to herself. In preparation she dressed herself in a nice housedress but after looking at her frizzy hair, she plopped on her head an old red wig, which she got on backwards and off to the side, the wig resembling a hairy football helmet tilted sideways.

Although others on their way to chapel saw Olga and her hair problem, they said nothing as she was not one to take suggestions, the latter perceived as criticisms. Olga

Wine is fine, but liquor is quicker . . .

was not to be trifled with.

The church services began and all went well and proper in the early segments. There were the three Bible readings, followed by the standard twenty-minute sermon which she may or may not have listened to. She had told her table partners at supper one time that one of the few advantages of being hard of hearing was the ability to literally turn off boring speakers.

After the message and a hymn came the planned liturgical service preceding communion, a liturgy Olga could follow along word for word as it was printed in their new green hymnal and service book. (She hated that dad-blamed green thing and fought the losing battle to bring back the old black one, and the **Concordia.**)

All was fine and proper — and quiet — in the church just before the actual distribution of the elements. At last the pastor, referred to by all as "that nice young man," asked the ushers to escort the members row by row to the altar to receive the bread and wine, and members were asked to leave their service books in the pews.

Therein may have been the problem. When Olga had the words to follow along with, she appeared comfortable and seemed both rational and cooperative. Her book now lay back in the pew.

By the time Olga shuffled up to the altar and knelt down on the kneeling cushion, all comfort, reason and cooperation were about to disappear.

The pastor, carrying a small silver tray of thin wafers, was walking slowly past each kneeling figure, each with an open hand out to receive the wafer. To each communicant the pastor murmured softly, "This is the body of Christ."

When the pastor got to Olga's station there was no open hand but a clenched fist. Nevertheless, he said gently to her, "This is the body of Christ."

"WHAT'S THAT?" shouted Olga. "SPEAK UP LOUDER."

Taken back just slightly, the pastor did repeat the line more loudly.

"Ya talk like ya got your mouth full of jelly-beans!! I can't unnerstand a word you're saying. STOP MUMBLING!"

"THIS IS THE BODY OF CHRIST!"

"Oh. It is? You sure?" And Olga accepted a wafer but then carefully examined it. "Hey, mister, I thought we were s'posed to get bread. This don't look like the whole-wheat kind we used to get back in our country church," but she did put the wafer in her mouth and the minister slid quickly along to the other kneelers.

By this point, of course, the rest of the congregation was aghast. Handkerchiefs were clenched, stomachs tightened, and bodies squirmed. Worse, they all knew what was coming next, namely receiving the communion wine. What would happen then? What words would Olga come out with next?

With the bread distributed, the pastor turned and placed the wafer-tray down. Now would come to each kneeler the distribution of a tiny glass of wine. The pastor picked up a large tray of filled glasses and started down along the row proclaiming quietly to each person the prescribed words: "This is the blood of Christ," as he handed a glass to each one.

At this moment most of the congregation hoped that the still-kneeling Olga would get skipped over, but the pastor never hesitated when he came to Olga. He leaned down towards her and stated the line very clearly, or so it seemed to the whole church.

"How's that again?" asked Olga. "SPEAK UP SO A PERSON CAN HEAR!"

"THIS IS THE BLOOD OF CHRIST!"

"REALLY! BLOOD!? YUK! CANNIBALS!" yelled Olga. The congregation about died.

Yet the minister never flinched. He responded with a theological position and explanation: "As Martin Luther stated, the wine has within it changes. Just like putting a metal rod into fire, the rod remains metal and yet it is altered, changed by the heat of the fire. Thus too is Christ within the wine."

"Is it really wine, then?" asked Olga, and the pastor

seemed relieved to answer a quick if qualified Yes. Things seemed in control again.

They weren't. Olga chose that moment to add, "Well, as my Pa used to say, 'Wine is fine but liquor is quicker.' "

Audible groans came from every nervous person in the chapel. The fidgeting organist considered quickly playing The Star Spangled Banner, with the hope that everyone would stand up, and then flee the place.

The nice young man in vestments, however, never lost his cool, and he said carefully and deliberately to Olga: "Let me come to your room and talk to you about all this after the services end today."

And that Olga heard and that Olga liked. Visitors were too few and far between to be turned down., And just maybe she understood more than indicated as she smiled at that nice young man and gave him a little wink and the pastor winked back.

Olga reached out her hand and accepted the tiny vessel holding the port wine and for half a second the congregation held its breath expecting Olga to raise the glass high and declare "Down the hatch!" but she didn't. She took a little sip, returned the glass, stood up and returned to her pew. It was all over.

It had been quite a communion service that day in the nursing home chapel, one that the participants and the townspeople would never forget, alas.

Mobility:
Southern Snowbirds
and Tucson Transplants

Among the most remarkable changes between those years around World War II and the present time is the extraordinary mobility of people. Americans are on the move everywhere.

This highly mobile society is taken for granted nowadays by younger people. They're used to long trips and longer vacations taking them by plane, train or car to Anywhere, USA.

Older people today, however, can still sit back and shake their heads in amazement at how different — and easy, and accepted — traveling is today compared to their yesterdays.

Senior citizens can easily recall when any trip over 100 miles was an adventure and maybe a once-in-childhood experience. To drive out of state used to be regarded as a major challenge to family planning and finances, plans requiring weeks of preparations.

And to travel out of the country, well, that was considered beyond the realm of reality for all except the world's millionaires! London was about as accessible to most Americans as the moon.

Going-to-Europe heretofore was something most Americans saw done only in the movies, so if one paid the twenty-five cent adult ticket fee, one could look up on the silver screen and vicariously join The Rich as they boarded the next luxury ocean liner to exotic foreign ports. Only Spencer Tracy and Katherine Hepburn went abroad in real life as well as reel life.

Times have changed. Both interstate and international

traveling are commonplace. This easy-access-to-anywhere includes those Northerners on near-whim who hustle South just to avoid the snow-season. It's all so easy and accepted, and to many, expected, to head South in the wintertime. What would their ancestors say about this?

What the true immigrants themselves would have said about the I-35s and the I-25s leading to Arizona, Texas and Florida is beyond comprehension. Presumably the immigrants would have found it incomprehensible to envision thousands of citizens fleeing snow-flakes.

We do know that the children and the grandchildren of immigrants head out in larger numbers every year for the cactus country, leaving just ahead — they hope — of their state's first big snowstorm. Some folks seem almost like winter lemmings in their response to the pull of nature towards deserts and mountains and sage brush — and that warm-warm-warm sunshine.

Of course the changing economic good times for millions of citizens now floating somewhere in that Great Middle Class designation have permitted them to have summer all winter long. If you've got the bucks, the green grass and flowers are waiting for you in January. Just get in the family vehicle and go!

The interstate highway system literally represents the cars of the entire nation and not only those of the state where the four-laner happens to be in.

Around the New Year the extra cars and campers and trailers, especially "trailers" — recreational vehicles/RVs — represent a moving flood of pale-skinned "foreigners" seeking sunshine and the blue skies found in the American Southwest.

The Southwest states are not about to forget why all the "company" is arriving and their media remind everyone of the reasons. Most daily newspapers everywhere have a little blip on the front page to indicate the weather for that day, but the Southwest newspapers carry this news as a major world event! They really lay on the puffery, like these samples from the **Arizona Daily**

Star: "Go ahead, Grand and Glorious Southern Arizona Sunshine. Make our Day — Again." Also: "Ho Hum, Just Another Beautiful Warm January Day."

Southwest television stations emphasize and re-emphasize their own weather compared with the climate "Up North." Weather reporters practically drool all over the screen as they contrast the warmth of their region compared to Siberia, by which is meant any state north of Oklahoma. A snow and ice-storm anywhere makes Southwest TV reporters gleeful; they don't smile at their weather maps, they leer.

Those visitors arriving with salt brine on their cars picked up in Des Moines or Omaha or Points North are collectively given the name of Snow Birds by Southwesterners, a term that is mainly neutral in connota-tion. No negative bias is necessarily implied in the phrase Snow Bird.

Yet Chambers of Commerce envision beautiful dollar signs when they hear the phrase, while a few others view the northerners as Invaders rather than free-spending Tourists, hence bumper stickers are available which read: "Welcome To Arizona. Now Turn Around and Go Home."

Alas, for the xenophobes living in the cactus country, the Snow Birds won't disappear until about May 1 when the reverse migration begins. The I-35s get extra busy again. It's time to go home.

But not all people go back north, of course. Contrary to what seems peculiar to Yankees, people actually live in Arizona all year around, although the Snow Birds wonder why.

The more people get acquainted with each other in Arizona who live there all year, the more one wonders if anyone was actually born and raised in that state. And if the person were indeed a "native," that is, born there, it seems certain that that person's parents were "immigrants."

And when does Arizona become "home?" In lengthy

conversations with two retired people who both coincidentally moved to Tucson in 1946 and have lived there since, both persons (who would marry in 1961) spoke fondly of "up North" and "back home," and carried it farther, "back home on the farm." Truly, the country was still very much in the souls of these two transplants from Wisconsin.

These Tucson transplants said, however, that if they lived in Arizona another hundred years, they still would not find cactus or rocks and gravel — even green gravel — acceptable for lawns. They added that the majestic saguaro cactus plant, the symbol of the state, still couldn't supersede the beauty of a plain blue spruce tree "back home."

The tortilla shells available everywhere may be made of potatoes and corn and flour, but despite the color and the texture, back-home lefse they were not.

These Arid-zona Northerners indicated that Christmas was the most difficult time for adjustment because Santa without snow was like, well, like lutefisk without lefse — and neither food was available in the land where tacos outsell hot-beef sandwiches ten to one.

And so the ex-Wisconsinites spoke longingly of "back home on the farm," of green wooded hillsides, of meandering creeks through lowland swamps, of the smell of fresh clover during the haying seasons.

But when the glaze left their eyes and nostalgia was set aside, neither one had the slightest intention of ever moving back north again. "North" is a place to visit in June, July and August.

Home is where the heart is? Perhaps home is where the heat is.

Arizona Aliens

One after another they hustled quickly through the restaurant door to beat the rest of the church-going-crowd also planning to eat noon-hour lunch.

The two dozen or so adult men and women moved briskly to the large table back in the corner so that they could all be together. Before even asking for menus, coffee was ordered all around.

They were a noisy bunch as they pulled out their chairs and moved themselves up to the table, but the noise was only that of friendly conversation as everyone was animatedly talking to everyone else.

What made their conversation stand out — aside from the volume — was the Norwegian language being spoken by some, along with heavily accented English delivered by others. The conversations flew wildly in Norsk and near-Norsk.

There was enough interest in this special group so that the manager came out from the kitchen to see and hear for himself what was going on back in the corner of his restaurant in Tucson, Arizona, on this January Sunday.

After listening a little while, he whispered to a customer at the counter whom he knew and asked what language it was that these people were talking, and he was informed it was Norwegian.

At this point the manager concluded that here indeed was another group of foreigners visiting America, and apparently he viewed it as proper for himself to bid a personal welcome to these guests from a Scandinavian nation.

The manager walked up to the table, har-umphed properly to get their attention, and pulled himself up to his full height, gestures that caused all at the table to stop talking and turn towards the man about to make them a short speech:

"On behalf of this restaurant management, and speaking somewhat for all of us good people here in Tucson, I want to welcome all of you warmly to our country and hope that you enjoy your stay in our land."

At these lines the people at the table began to look at each other with questioning glances. No one said anything for several seconds: there was an awkward moment of embarrassment, and finally a large man at the end of the table looked up at the manager and said:

"Vell, we want to t'ank you very much, but that vussn't vreally necessary. Ve're all from Crookston, MinneSOHta."

Shoes, Swedes, And Marital Strain

A pair of shoes. A plain pair of women's shoes. That doesn't seem very important, but shoes can mean the difference between going out and staying home, between working in the house or outside the home.

Shoes can also become a prime factor between a wife's idea of a job and a husband's notion about wives' working.

* * * *

Gunder Hedberg was an emigrant Swede who came to America in the 1920's and took up the trade of carpentry. Gunder possessed a strong back and a strong will, traits that were an integral part of the young man, the latter trait especially being highly significant. On certain ideas and opinions, Gunder would not budge one inch. A stubborn Swede. A dour Swede.

In America, Gunder was both surprised and annoyed by the changes he saw compared to his homeland, changes notably in the role of American women. Women here did not do field work, did not do barn work, did not tend the cattle, all work commonly done by females back in the old country.

American women didn't wear old-world clothes, didn't serve old-world foods except for special holidays. They drank too much coffee and ate too much pork. And they didn't scrub the floors each week.

These changes Gunder was able to tolerate in part; on these things he could budge a little. But the overall idea that it was the man who went outside the home and earned a living while the woman stayed home, took care of the house and raised the children — that belief was not even an issue to be argued or even discussed. Some things are plain as the nose on the face.

Gunder believed solidly that a wife belongs at home. Period. That was that. Such a basic position was engraved in his mind as firmly and clearly as though the message was carved on some runestone.

Gunder would eventually marry an intelligent, attractive American lady. The timing of their marriage, however, corresponded to the timing of the Great American Depression. Carpentry jobs were few and far between. Hard times for the newlyweds.

For reasons both economic and personal, the new wife was determined to get a job somewhere, anywhere. This decision seemed reasonable enough to her, but not to her husband. The ensuing go-arounds between the two found neither person budging. And despite the husband's adamant stand on this matter, the wife rebelled. She went out and did find a job. However, the job lasted less than one day, all because of a pair of shoes.

With the husband at work, the wife had gone out and answered an advertisement for a position as a hostess in a restaurant near their home. Dressed to the nines, wearing her best dress and her only pair of good shoes, the employer who interviewed her was so favorably impressed that he hired her immediately, the work to begin the next day.

That night there was another argument, the husband still unmoving from his original position. He added more reasons. Not only was it morally wrong for the wife to go out off the house to work, it was an absolute insult to her husband! Such a move on the wife's part was a clear and open statement to the world that the husband could not provide for his own family. And that kind of insult he would not tolerate!

In his view, the only acceptable work-for-pay for a wife was to do some work that could be done in the home — and only in the home. He thus allowed her to take in washing, a gesture of magnanimous compromise, he believed. She would have none of it. Thus an impasse,

She could not leave the house without shoes on . . .

with no resolution reached by midnight. Two angry people went off to bed.

Next morning the husband got up early, as usual, packed his lunch, as usual, and left for work before dawn. The wife was also up early to get herself ready for her own job, but not arising until she heard the click of the front door, indicating her spouse was gone.

She soon got herself fixed up and dressed very nicely and was ready to leave; then came the crucial problem. She could not find her shoes. She hunted everywhere, combing the upstairs, downstairs and even the basement, but no shoes were to be found.

Weary, she removed her gloves, her hat and her coat and sat down. Obviously she could not leave the house without shoes on. She did not go to work that day, nor the next day, nor the following days; indeed not ever.

(The next week she did kind of "go" to work; she took in dirty laundry — at home.)

As to the missing shoes? Her husband had taken them that first morning, put them in his lunch pail, and walked out the door. He would win. His plan was fool-proof.

Years later, as aging couples got together with friends and talked about the old days and acknowledged certain problems and obstacles in their early married years, Gunder would laugh uproariously as he regaled his audience about the shoe-story.

But even years later, no matter how often that story got told and retold, only one of the marriage partners would find the tale amusing.

The Waspish Wisdom of the Aged

The tall, bony, bent lady was both spry and sharp for her age, 85. "A tough old gal," agreed the men in front of the hardware store who watched her come walking briskly to town every morning with her shopping bag. "A smart lady, too," they added.

Given both her energy and intellect,as well as her advanced years, Amelia Nottleson was a kind of institution in town. Because she had lived there all her life, she was virtually a pioneer, and so anyone who wanted to know any history of the community came to see Amelia. The results were mixed.

Amelia might talk to them, and then again she might not, depending on her mood at the moment. Because she could at times be brusque in her manner, some people were a bit afraid of her. "An independent cuss," added the hardware store men of Amelia.

Widowed for a quarter of a century, Amelia lived on the edge of the village in a small house which she kept immaculately clean. Her yard was as clean as her house. If there was one trait brought over from Norway by this emigrant lady, it was cleanliness.

And new-fangled contraptions she avoided, useless things like indoor toilets. At age 85 Amelia was still taking the early morning walk to the biffy out in back, rain or shine, summer or winter. ("Thunder mugs" under the bed took care of indoor night needs.)

It was both her age and home conditions that brought her daughter, age 65, also widowed, to come to live with Amelia and help her and take care of her, all things the mother found totally unnecessary and a bit presumptuous on the daughter's part.

It was this situation of elderly daughter coming to live with aged mother that would give rise to one of the better one-liners that circulated through town, which line at the same time reinforced the image of the ruggedness of Amelia and her possible immortality. (Because it was the daughter who relayed the mother's remark at church circle, there is no question of the authenticity of the tale.)

It seems that Amelia was looking into — but no more than making discreet inquiry — the remote possibility of having someday to move to a retirement center or nursing home.

When this inquiry was inadvertently made known to the daughter, Amelia was informed that she, her daughter, would take very good care of her mother and that Amelia need not worry about the future.

It was to this statement of well-meant reassurance that Amelia responded, first with a snort of disdain before adding her great line: "Well, I can't be too careful about the years ahead. After all, you won't live forever, you know."

For photograph of Amelia, see page 196

Check the Menu First

Strangers who drive off the highway to eat at small town restaurants can sometimes be in for a big food surprise. The shock can be either pleasant or awful, depending on how one views the culinary results lying on a plate in front of the customer. Food can be amazing and amusing, and certainly there is a lesson to be learned, as might be concluded from this particular experience.

The lesson began when this strange car pulled up in front of the tiny cafe, The Norske Nook. The car indeed was strange in that all the local patrons sitting inside this Scandinavian restaurant looked up and agreed that they had never seen that particular vehicle before on main street.

And the locals knew all the local cars, and the pick-ups, too, including the added knowledge on how each ran, along with their gas mileage. They even knew which ones were financed and which ones were paid for!

So into the cafe this Sunday noon hour walked the new couple who chose naturally to sit at the farthest table from the counter, where every stool was occupied. Soon waitress Kari Gurholt, a bouncy high school girl who worked there on weekends, dashed over with two glasses of water in plastic glasses along with two well-worn menus enclosed in plastic folders. The stage was being set.

After briefly studying the bill-o-fare — and mumbling in amazement at the low prices — the customers chose the Day's Special, a ham dinner with boiled potatoes and boiled cabbage and boiled carrots, all foods topped with a mound of butter which melted all over the large, heavy plate. A solid meal, a local favorite, food that would stick to the ribs. Mmmmmmm, good — and lots of it.

Afterwards, when they finished, the bouncing Kari flitted over to their table to scoop up their dirty plates, and she blithely inquired: "Wouldja like some dessert, then?"

Yes, the man allowed, he would like some dessert. In fact, he said, "I'd like to order a Cherry Heering sundae."

The waitress stopped wiggling. She stood very still and got a puzzled look on her face, believing she had heard wrong.

"Whadja say?"

"A Cherry Heering ice cream sundae, please."

"Yah," murmured Kari, very perplexed, "that's what I thought ya said,"

The bewilderment was obvious as Kari now ambled slowly back towards the counter. She stopped, screwed up her face, then chose to go to the cash register up front to consult with her boss. After a whispered conversation, with headshaking by the twosome, both parties together went into the kitchen where they brought in a third consultant, the hefty cook, and soon the three of them came out by the counter scratching their heads and looking frequently at the back table where this curious food order had started.

Some thirty seconds of quiet discussion ended with all nodding in agreement, and the trio dispersed to their former places. Kari went to work on the order. After an initial stop at the ice cream freezer came a trip back to the refrigerator and finally a pause to get a small jar out of a back cupboard. She then made the sundae.

Her mission accomplished, her order filled, Kari was back in bouncing form and so she swooped once more back to the customer's table where she placed before him a large soup bowl filled with the ingredients.

In front of the surprised customer sat the order, or the order perceived by the meeting of three consultants. Lying there in the middle of the bowl was a large scoop of vanilla ice cream which was surrounded by a neat, complete circle of twelve chunks of pickled herring. On top of the ice cream lay one red cherry.

The moral of this story is simple: only order off the menu.

How (not) to Establish Family Traditions

It is important to maintain family traditions. Some families work hard to promote ongoing traditions while others don't even consciously try. Yet, either way, their offspring grow up with memories of "the way we did it at home when we were kids."

Within these same family traditions, it is just as important to maintain ethnic heritage at the same time. Kids need to know their ethnic background. "Know ye the rock from which you were hewn," wrote the prophet Isaiah, "the quarry from which you were digged."

(I have a messianic complex on the need for people to know their heritage and regularly through the years have done "missionary work" with my students so that they will know their roots.)

Preserving and promoting traditions and heritage can, however, be a difficult problem. At least for our family it was tough, and that problem is the subject of this article.

Most American ethnicity comes out at Christmas time. With Santa-season also comes heritage time, often in the form of ethnic foods. We are what we eat. For Scandinavians, Christmas brings out from the kitchen fattigman, krumkake, rosettes, spritz, romegrot, and other ethnic foods. One eats one's heritage at Christmas time. (If you don't know your ethnic background between Christmas and New Year's, the cook in the kitchen has failed you.)

For many older Scandinavians today, especially those with Norwegian backgrounds, the great majority can recall that in their childhood their families always but always had lutefisk and lefse for Christmas Eve supper. For both my wife Judy and myself, lutefisk and lefse was our childhood tradition, too, on Christmas Eve. (The fact that I didn't like it as a kid had nothing to do with our decision-making later, alas.)

After consultation on the importance of heritage, we concluded definitely that that was one important tradition that must be passed on to the next generation, our children. Yes, lutefisk and lefse was both the answer and the solution. Then would our offspring know their heritage, then would they be proud of their ancestry, their immigrant forefathers; then would they become better citizens themselves because of this knowledge, this honorable tradition.

Three cheers for lutefisk and lefse! Our family genes and genealogy would carry on forever — or so we naively thought. However, it was not only a mistake, it was a disaster.

Normally, small children look forward to Christmas Eve like no other night of the year. That's normal in normal houses, but to our three children, normal houses should not be stunk up at holly-time with the smell of rotten fish, or so they proclaimed in wailing voices.

Worse. Not only did they have to smell it, they had — absolutely HAD — to eat it! Well, at least one little bite. So amid pinched noses and gagging and yuks and threats to report the cruelty of their parents to the police, we did indeed have lutefisk and lefse for several Christmas Eves.

Christmas Eve, of course, should not be spoiled by anything, let alone the results of ethnic heritage in the form of a jiggling white, pasty, glutinous fish that afterwards left the silverware blackened and the children nauseated. What kind of childhood remembrances would that produce? They'd hate their Scandinavian heritage if they were force-fed lutefisk once a year. It was time for a change.

More consultation between husband and wife (us), and the obvious conclusion that a new food must be substituted on Christmas Eve, but it must be ethnic! So what other meals do Scandinavians serve? Oysters. That's it! Oyster stew. Fresh oysters cooked in hot milk and served in soup bowls along with little oyster-crackers. Yummy! And the kids will love it!

They didn't love it. They hated oysters more than lutefisk. And though not premeditated, the kids got their revenge, of sorts, that made for yet one more meal substitution.

On that Christmas Eve we first served oyster stew — that one night when all the fancy of the fancy dishes and silverware and goblets come out of storage for their annual appearance — it was the same old fight at the table:

"I hate it!"

"It's really very good. Try a little more. It'll grow on you."

"Eeeeeee-yuk! They're slimy and ishy."

"Just eat the milk, then."

"It tastes like dish water. Barfy!"

"You've got to try some."

"I won't."

"You will. YOU WILL! OR YOU WON'T GET TO OPEN YOUR PRESENTS!"

The latter was the ultimate threat that worked every time, cruel and unfair that it might have been. And so all three kids gagged some oyster stew down, all the time proclaiming: "I know I'm gonna get sick." This was more than an idle comment.

Christmas Eve traditions also included midnight church services. So, after the oyster-stew-fight, and after all the dishes were washed and put away, of course, and after the family's small program around the tree, a program which always included carol singing and the father reading the Christmas gospel from St. Luke, and after the presents finally got to be ripped open and oohed and awwwed over, the family members eventually crawled into the cold car late at night and headed off to the midnight church services, the kids STILL grumbling about their poor stomachs and those awful oysters. Not to worry, said the parents.

Both my wife and I sing in the choir, and so we sat in the choir loft up front while the kids, after promising solemnly not to fight, sat side by side in a pew about halfway back. Ah, tradition. The atmosphere in church on Christmas Eve is lovely. At least it is supposed to be lovely. The church was dark and so still, and there was a spotlight on the pastor as he mounted the pulpit to begin the sermon.

About halfway through the minister's message, there was suddenly a loud commotion somewhere out in the congregation, followed by whispers and stirring and shuffling, moving bodies. Something was obviously wrong.

The pastor went right on talking, however, paying no attention to the brief disturbance in the pews. About two minutes later the door directly across from the choir opened, and there in the doorway stood our nine-year-old daughter, Kristen, with a stricken look on her face. With eyes popping, she was mouthing some words at us, words we couldn't quite make out at the time, but we nodded anyway, as much for her to close the door as to acknowledge the message.

Only after the services ended and we went downstairs to the fellowship room and saw this small group of people standing around some tiny figure supine on a table did we sense that the problem upstairs had been moved downstairs, and the problem was ours.

There stretched out on her back was our five-year-old daughter, Karin, lying lifeless, her face as white as a sheet, her red hair in striking contrast to her ashen appearance. She looked as though the embalmer had already arrived.

"She got sick in church," said twelve-year-old son, Scott, something we had by then pretty well figured out. "Wow! Did she ever heave!" he added, a bit unnecessarily, a full description not really wanted.

Now came the children's revenge. While the rest of the congregations had long left the sanctuary, my wife and I were still on our hands and knees at one a.m. underneath the pews upstairs, with pails of water and rags, cleaning up the mess. And it was a mess, the oysters having cleaned her out totally — and distributed broadly throughout the middle of the church. Small wonder the commotion it caused.

Afterwards we wrapped "the body" in a blanket, carried her out to the parking lot on this bitter cold snowy Christmas Eve, and we drove silently homeward, everyone there knowing full well that that would be one family experience they'd never forget. (And they haven't.) Nor would there be any more oyster stew or lutefisk or lefse.

Since that fateful night we have had a pork-roast on Christmas Eves. It just takes a little bold experimentation before finding the right ethnic traditions to pass on to the next generation.

Normal houses should not be stunk up
at holly-time with the smell of rotten fish . . .

AMELIA NOTTLESON (p. 187)
and JULIA LEE (p. 61)

LARS LEE, the emigrant from Norway in 1878, who came as Lars Lioien. Left. A Lee family (c. 1940) on the Lars Lee farm in Decorah, Iowa. Seated: Arthur, Sr, Lars (p. 61). Standing: Robert, Julia, Madelyn and Art (author of book). For family-trips to farm, see *Leftover Lutefisk,* p. 47; on Julia, p. 76; on Lars, p. 129.

LOREN "Lars" LEE
(As WWII soldier and photo today; see p. 52)

(For family photos see *Lutefisk,* pg. 219, 220)

JOHN MOE
(story on page 148)

SAM HELLUM, "The King of Town Characters," in the Lutefisk Ghetto, the author's hometown. (See p. 17; also there's frequent references to Sam in **The Lutefisk Ghetto,** e.g. p. 23.) Both Sam's social life (above) and his working life, such as it was, (left) are viewed in the select objects of each photo, namely The Beer and The Ax. Note also Sam's wearing of his Eisenhower jacket from a war that would save Sam's life eventually. In the 1980s, the charitable might label Sam a "free spirit"; in the 70s he was "an individualist"; in the 60s he'd be a "pre-hippy"; but in the 40s and 50s—his heydays—he was just a wonderful, wacky character. Yup yup yup.

THE AUTHOR'S CHILDREN, as pictured at different stages and ages, and semi-featured in final story (p. 191). Left: Scott, Kristen (standing) and Karin, in somewhat recent photo. Above: Same crew as caught (forced to pose) unhappily before rushing off for first day of a new school year (circa 1972). The first-day-of-school photo-taking was repeated every year, providing they could be rounded up and made to stand still two seconds. Bottom Left: Karin as red-haired, freckled-faced kid who was the major "victim" of Christmas foods in the story—EAT IT! OR YOU WON'T GET TO OPEN ANY PRESENTS!—about Ethnic Heritage literally forced down the throats of reluctant, rebellious children. At the time of this publication, however, Scott, 31, teaches in a private school in Mexico; Kristen, 28, (now Mrs. Rick Barnes) is a physical education teacher in a Seattle elementary school; Karin, 24, is a graduate student in Scandinavian Studies at the University of Washington. (And they all still hate lutefisk.)